SUNSHINE AND SHADOWS

with

WILLIAM D. GALE

Other Books by William D. Gale

I Sat Where They Sat

The Loving Shepherd: The Lost Sheep

Miss Winnie Crouch • *A Heroine of the Faith*

Amazing Grace Church Hymnal (Philippine) • *English words and music – Ilocono words*

Happy Happenings (Coming Soon)

Through

SUNSHINE AND SHADOWS

with

WILLIAM D. GALE

REVIVALIST PRESS
Cincinnati, Ohio

Through Sunshine and Shadows with William D. Gale
An Autobiography

ISBN 0-9749186-0-1

Published by Revivalist Press
publishing ministry of

God's Bible School & College
1810 Young Street
Cincinnati, OH 45202
Revivalist@gbs.edu

Printed by Country Pines, Inc., Shoals, Indiana
United States of America

CONTENTS

APPRECIATION

To numerous friends who encouraged me to write my life story.

To Alice Kathryn, my wife, who spent untold hours typing nearly the entire hand-written manuscript on her word processor; correcting, punctuating and spelling.

To Dr. Michael Avery who prepared Chapter 14 and gave many helpful suggestions.

To Brenda Herring for her special assistance in preparing the manuscript.

To Mandy Mimier for retyping the manuscript in computer type for printing.

DEDICATION

Across many years of travel in our ministry of evangelism and missionary work, we have been privileged to stay in the homes of pastors and laymen. We have enjoyed the hospitality of many friends in our fifty states and other lands. We have often said that we could travel a day's journey any direction and stay with our family or friends. It is to all of you that we wish to dedicate this life story.

Foreword

Some lives are lived for God so well that their story merits telling. Such is the life of William D. Gale. The journey begins in a sod house on the plains of Nebraska and winds through sixty years of active ministry. The story will let you relive his childhood and watch the amazing transformation of a mischievous farm boy into a missionary statesman. You will be challenged as you read how a childlike faith moved the hand of God to do the miraculous. But best of all you will feel the passion of a man who wrapped his arms around lost humanity and loved them one by one to Christ. Whether on a Native American reservation, in a remote mountain village in the Philippines, or in a mud hut in Mexico, no place was too far, no trail too rugged, and no life too hopeless for him to take the wonderful news of redeeming grace. As you read *Through Sunshine and Shadows*, you will see the story of William D. Gale is really *His* story.

Dr. Michael R. Avery, President

God's Bible School and College

Preface

When a small lad, I learned that Dr. Hubble had come to our home to care for Mother and me when I was born. Our home was built from sod. It was located four to five miles east of US Highway 83, two miles south of Lincoln-Logan County Line and almost directly south of Gandy. Our mailing address was Stapleton, Nebraska.

This area is known as Sandhill Country. It covers most of the north central part of the state. For many years our home was a historical sight. It was one of the last soddies in the nation and was known as the Gale Sod House. Now you have the location of my birth place in mind, but if you decide to go there you had better wait until after a rain. It is easy to get stuck in dry sand; even worse than mud since it has no bottom.

At a recent Gale Family Reunion, my wife and I, some of my siblings, our son and two daughters drove out to see the old home place. The buildings were all gone, of course, but Alice and Aleta found more rusty stuff than you can imagine. They brought some of it back to North Platte where the family was gathered and decorated the tables with it. The girls sold a roll of rusty wire at $1.00 a foot as a memorial. We had lots of fun. Aleta drove back out later and dug up two sand roses. One has lived. She will want you to see it, but guards it with a club.

If you get stuck in the sand when you come out to the old home place, phone me and I'll tell you how to let some of the air out of your tires so they'll cushion out and pull better. Be sure to have a tire pump with you if you do this.

I have been requested many times over the years to write my life story. Finally, I am endeavoring to do so. I have edited over 100 accounts of Happy Happenings. I hope to collect most of these into book form.

They contain some miraculous events. When these are in print, they will be a good companion to my life story.

My exposure to Indian people and their way of life has been meaningful to me. Many of my dearest and closest friends are Indians. This has helped to build a heartthrob for world missions. Serving on several missions boards has increased the burden even more.

My prayer is that those who read this book will come to know my Savior in a deeper commitment. He has so wonderfully changed my life and given me a heart of love for missions. This book represents a strong effort to remember interesting and special happenings. We welcome you to travel with us *Through Sunshine and Shadows.*

William D. Gale

1

Childhood Memories

William and Model T Ford

*T*he year was 1920, so I'm told. The place was in the sod house on Great Uncle Hugh's ranch. This was about ten miles southeast of Stapleton, Nebraska and about two miles south of the Lincoln County line where I, William Duane Gale, was born, so I am told. My parents were William Britt and Cynthia Wilson Gale, so I'm told. I want to be honest and that's before my memory worked very well, but I was there, so I'm told. My earliest memories are while Great Uncle Tom was rolling me back and forth in my buggy and he pulled it over his sore toe. Now I don't want anyone to call me a liar, please. I don't honestly remember much about the buggy, but I do remember how Uncle Tom acted and hollered. It may help you to better believe this when you remember some of us Gales slept in the buggy until we were nearly ready to shave.

Since my memories almost create an autobiography, I am dividing them under three categories. For this reason they are not given in chronological sequence. First, Astonishing Things, second, Amusing Things, and finally, Amazing Things.

Astonishing Things

In those days, I couldn't have built an outhouse, let alone a house. One of my first astonishments was the sod house where I was born. Little did I realize then how unusual it was to be born in a "Little Old Sod Shanty on the Claim." Really, the reason I remember it so well was that even the folks spoke of the sod house with a bit of surprise.

Another of our buildings I remember was our big hay barn. In this connection, I remember when Kenneth showed me how a tough guy could light a match and set the hay on fire and smother it with his fist. The next big thing I remember was when I tried to show Pat how a tough guy could do it. My first mistake was to try it; the second was to pick a windy day. I lit the match all right, but, oh, how it burned my fist! The barn burned fast. We got the horses and stock out, but forgot until too late about the harnesses and saddles. I guess I should call this memory, "The Whipping I Didn't Get." The neighbors came in for miles to help move the big stack of hay. The barn burned to the ground and the manure pile burned for three weeks. I remember so well how so many asked, "How did it happen?" Mom didn't answer. Uncle Doc asked if Lady burned up, and then my big tough uncle began to cry. I found a big club. When I gave it to Dad, I said, "Please beat me to death, I did it." Both my Dad and Uncle Doc had arrived home with a load of cattle and Dad said that they would likely winter kill. Oh, how I wished for a licking! He didn't do it, but then he cried, too, which was worse.

Not everything that happened to me was sad. I remember some cold days when we all stood around the cook stove trying to keep warm and eat our breakfast. The astonishing thing was how you could get so hot in front and so cold on the back side. The syrup even boiled in our tin plates as we sat around the edge of the stove while Mother fried more flapjacks. One of my boyhood memories and marvels was how they could jack up the back wheel of the Model T Ford and make it easier to crank. Sometimes when that didn't work, we'd push it down hill and back up hill, so we could push it down again. It was the most sure way to start it. Once when Dad was trying to crank it, Mother kept asking questions: "Daddy, did you try this; Daddy, did you try that?" The car didn't get hot, but Dad did. You could just about see blue smoke as he swore and sent Mother to the house. She just got in and shut the door and the car started. When Mother came back, she and Dad laughed. He said, "If I had known that would start it, I'd have sent you in a long time ago."

I was really proud of Dad when he put a valve system in the gas tank lid and pumped air in the tank so we wouldn't have to back over some steep hills. He wouldn't let Kenneth and me tell what he had done. Model T Fords had a gravity feed and the neighbors thought we had the most powerful Model T in the country.

I not only marveled at Dad's skills, but at his long vision. He saw the corn silk smoke about half a mile from the house. He wouldn't raise boys that were sneaks, so he took us to the house and made us use his pipes and some real tobacco in front of him and Mom. Kenneth caught on to what he was doing and claimed to be too sick to smoke more than the first pipe full. I knocked the ashes out twice and said, "Fill it again, Dad." On the third pipe full, I got seasick, car sick, and tobacco sick all at the same time. I got so dizzy. I heaved up everything but my socks and was pulling hard on them. It was a long time before I tried to smoke again.

I was really more than astonished when the hair rubbed off the sides of the ponies when we bounced up and down as we rode them to school. Kenneth's horse showed only one bare spot. Lady showed two bare spots because Pat and I rode double. That's not what was so astonishing! The funny thing was how angry Uncle Doc acted when he found we were racing his horse Buck during the noon hour. Kenneth always rode! That's not so funny either. The astonishing and funny thing was the way Uncle Doc was mad at us but bragged to everyone else that his horse was the fastest of them all and won all the races.

Amusing Things!

Some of the things I just mentioned weren't funny. At least we didn't laugh when they happened, or at least not much anyhow. Something that wasn't amusing, but Mother would have been real unhappy if we didn't add this to our memories, were the magic words, "castor oil." Three tablespoons of castor oil with a wee drop of orange juice to alter the taste counteracted all internal problems. This is the real reason us children were all so healthy. We all got our dosages at the same time and quite regularly. Of course it took turpentine with sugar to get rid of worms. It was castor oil for the inside, but skunk grease or goose grease applied to the outside for all external diseases.

Those were sad days when we left the sand hills. I remember how I felt when we drove the cattle miles to their new home after Dad sold them. We had ridden them all. They were kind of personal friends. Why shouldn't we be sad? The saddest things were when I got two big blisters from riding so far. I should have told you first, before we sold the cattle, how Kenneth broke the new yearly bull to ride. He was full of great ideas. The thing that was bad was that he thought I should carry them out.

Oh, yes, I started to tell you about the new bull Dad got. He could really buck. He would buck us off as fast as we got on. One day when the folks were gone, Kenneth got a super idea. We got the bull in the barn and tied him up to the manger. He didn't act as if he liked it. He acted even worse when I got on his back. He even bellowed some when Kenneth took the lariat rope and tied me on. I really didn't like the idea too much either. Kenneth was sure he could handle the situation so he tied me on good by wrapping ropes around and around me and the bull. He must have done a good job. Part of his plan was to let the bull loose. He would hold the halter rope and let him buck in the corral. His idea went quite well until he untied the halter rope and it slipped through his hands really fast. The bull hit the barn door and it flew open. The rodeo was on. That bull sure bucked. He even went over to the manure pile and threw manure all over me. Kenneth tried to rope him with another rope. When the bull tried to jump the gate, he got his feet caught in the wires. He stumbled and fell flat, belly down. How glad I am I was on the top side. He got up and bucked and ran out along the lane fence. He almost got into the barbed wires on both sides. It would have been hard on my legs if he had, because they were tied fast. Childhood memories! This is very vivid to me when that bull came bucking and running into the herd and they stampeded. The bull and I were in the middle of the herd. Oh, happy day and happy hour, the bull wore out and so did I. My nose bled; I mixed tears and blood together. When Kenneth rode up, the bull stood gently and let him untie me and take me off. He was gentle after that! And so was I. I bragged a little and said, "I rode him."

Just before we leave the ranch, just for sister Pat's sake, I should tell how in some acts of loving innocence she got me spanked. She had a big black umbrella. I could jump off the shed and the chicken house and hardly feel it because it cushioned the fall. Once when jumping off the high side of the toilet, Pat saw that the black umbrella got inverted. It actually turned inside out. I had an awful fall. Pat was unmindful of my wounded condition. She screamed as if something awful had happened and then told Mother how terrible it was. Mom seemed to know how bad she felt and unmindful of my broken body, gave me a real beating.

When we moved out to Wyoming and Colorado, lots of things happened that were both amazing and frustrating. We experienced living in a tent for a while. I remember two things about our neighbor's tent blowing down. I thought it looked so funny that I really laughed. When Mom came out to see what was so funny, she laughed because I was laughing. Dad came out to see what was so funny. He used some adjectives that are not proper, so I'll not repeat what he said, but he did give the impression he was not happy the way the wind was blowing, nor our laughing at the neighbor's calamity. He said ours would likely be the next tent to blow down.

Say, maybe I should tell you why I am like Abraham Lincoln. He lived in a log house and I lived in a sod house. It wasn't living in a log house that made the former president great, it was the fact that he got out of it. I got one over on him. He went to live in the white house; I went to live in a white tent.

The big day for us was when we got rich and moved back to North Platte and bought a Union Pacific boxcar. It was from there I went to start my Bible School career. Dad paid Rev. Chester Tulga, a holiness Baptist preacher, $75.00 for a lot and the boxcar. It was taken off the wheels and set on railroad ties. Dad took the sliding doors off and put in regular doors. Both had glass panes. Be it ever so humble, there is no place like home.

Don't rush me so fast. I want to stay out west long enough to tell you about Uncle John and Aunt Rose. I think they liked me; I sure did like them and I might mention that Aunt Rose was a champion cookie baker. You know, Uncle John could yell louder about nothing than any other man I ever knew. We got along so well they became my second "Mom and Dad."

I was going to tell you about the big fire in Berthoud, Colorado. Before getting right into the story, I should tell about some of my friends and me. We got a whole peck sack of brown corn silk. We took it up to the office of the beet dump for a little relaxed smoking. The beet dump was built so loaded trucks of sugar beets could be driven up a long ramp and emptied into a big chute that carried them into open railroad cars. The office was up there. We got to making big cigars, seeing who could puff the biggest cloud of smoke. That office room up there wasn't very big. It soon got so filled with smoke that we had to open the windows. It wasn't long after that when the fire whistle blew. That was exciting. We gave up our relaxation and ran down to the beet dump. When we looked back up at the office it really looked like it was on fire. We didn't realize we had created the big fire, but we kept on running until we got a long ways away. Fires are dangerous and we didn't want to get burned. Besides that, the fire trucks came to the beet dump.

The Rocky Mountain adventures ended when the folks decided to move back to North Platte, Nebraska. We lived in a small house behind Uncle Seeley's house. The top hadn't grown on his house yet. Out there one day Uncle Seeley got everyone he could to help carry a log. Cousin Clifford and I decided to carry a fence post and grunt like the rest. Uncle Seeley sure didn't know how to accept our joke. They had about done themselves in carrying the log, and he acted like we should have helped.

Aunt Bessie was really proud of her Buff Orpington chickens. Clifford and I decided we would help out in feeding them. We made one little mistake. We tied the kernels of corn to a string and the string to the fence. It was a little like catching fish, only more fun. We had nearly a dozen hens fastened to the strings. They were flapping and cackling at a great rate. Never saw anything funnier at a circus, until Aunt Bessie arrived and spoiled it all. She acted awful. It was terrible the way she spanked Clifford. She grabbed him first. It was disgraceful the way she treated him. I ran as fast as I could. I had to hide for a long time to keep down a terrible scandal.

Another shameful thing was the way Mom and Aunt Bessie would make us go to school even when our clothes were torn and we were terribly sick. That's another whole story. In my memories, I recall how Uncle Seeley complained about paying us for gardening when we took a few minutes off to write one of the best songs that was ever written. Alta Pearl helped us, but she was real religious and gave us most of the credit. You remember the old school song "Yankee Doodle." We used that tune. The third verse goes like this:

> Now all young girls who fall for us, and want to be true
> Just bake us up a chocolate cake, and we'll fall for you.

Chorus:
> Chocolate cake is our delight
> Chocolate cake is dandy
> Just bake us up a chocolate cake,
> And now and then some candy.

We had several stanzas. I wish I could remember them. My memories are more of the precious girls and the wonderful chocolate cakes. The little tokens of appreciation for our musical ability was almost overwhelming.

An amusing event took place in study period. Miss Heller came by my seat and said, "Singing in school time, young man, go to the office." I tried to explain to her that it was all a mistake, and that I was sorry. I explained that I was enjoying my schoolwork so much that I forgot myself. I even told her she was my favorite teacher and that I would never do it again. She wouldn't listen to good sound reasoning. She forced me to go when I knew she was making a mistake.

Mr. Killian talked awful rough to me. He told me to go back and behave. I was about to the door when Claren Goodwin entered. Mr. Killian enquired why he was there, and he said he laughed when Miss Heller sent William. He got his lecture, and as we were leaving, Glen Hardenbrook came in. His story was that he laughed when Miss Heller sent Glen to the office. Mr. Killian got all upset and called in all the teachers to witness our licking. He gave it to Claren first and he took it for he was tough. I took it, but I was not as tough.

When Glen bent over the chair and Mr. Killian came down with the strap on Glen's back section, he gave out a yell and jumped ten feet, carrying the chair with him. For the next few minutes we saw a real show. Mr. Killian would swing and miss; next time he would swing and hit. Finally Glen quit bending over the chair and just grasped his ankles. It was real funny to hear the strap sing up in the air. Glen would bow and jump like you wouldn't believe. All the teachers got to laughing, including Mr. Killian, but excluding Miss Heller. She got disgusted and decided to step in front of Glen. Mr. Killian got Glen with the end of the strap. Glen leaped, wrapped his legs and arms around Miss Heller and they piled into the corner. We all laughed. I got down on my knees and doubled over. I think it's the hardest I have ever laughed. I was trying to quit laughing, when Mr. Killian saw me. He said, "I don't think William has had enough." That sobered me up real quick. He let us go back to the room. He knew it was funny, too.

It would have been all right if I had kept the incident to myself. I couldn't wait, so I proceeded to tell the boy behind me. He started to study real quick. I turned around and got my geography book and went to studying. There was a deathly silence in that classroom. I studied long and hard. Finally, I tried to peek. Mr. Killian was still there. He motioned for me to come. I thought he had forgotten how to quit before he stopped the second time. This was my last school whipping.

Amazing Things

There are many supernatural things that happened in my life. If there is one above all others that has affected my life, it is the account of the Lord sending the folks home. It was when I was a small boy of 6 or 7 when it occurred. It is yet very vivid in my mind, although I may not have the details as accurate as I think. The folks would on occasions get up extra early to get the chores done, so they could get an early start to make the long 23 mile trip from our Sandhill home to North Platte. The old Model T had one door on the right side that opened. The other side was marked like a door but you had to crawl over. It had a small box on the back, which made it look like a coupe pickup. There was not much room in the front seat. Just enough for Dad, Mother and baby Darrell. The box would hold a can of cream, a crate of eggs and maybe a pig or calf for market. The legs of the animals had to be tied and the animals themselves tied down. The folks would promise us something good if we would be good and get the chores done. It might be an apple which we would eat core and all, unless we spit out seeds and stem. We ate the peelings and all if it were an orange. Sometimes it would be an all-day sucker, but it didn't last all day. We'd suck on in until it was all gone and then chew up the stick to get the sweet out of it.

Our chores were milking the cows, feeding the hogs, gathering eggs and getting the fuel. The fuel consisted of corn cobs and cow chips to burn. The cow chips never made much heat, but they did make a lot of ashes. Part of the way you got warm was by gathering them and carrying out the ashes. I have said for a long time that it was a funny country. The wind pumped the water and the cows cut the wood.

One summer day when the folks were gone to North Platte, the sky got real black. I got real frightened. It flashed lightning and clapped thunder real hard. Pat really got scared. I guess girls are like that. She ran to the house crying. I have said many times; shame on any boy who would let his sister cry and would not try to comfort her. When she ran to the house, I ran with her. Big brother Kenny came running, too. The lightning flashed, the thunder clapped and Pat crawled under the living room table.

Shame on any boy who would let his sister cry for the folks to come home, all by herself under the table. I got under the table to comfort her. It was even kind of big brother to get under there with us. I remember like yesterday how Pat cried for the folks to come home. Maybe you can't understand, but you can't comfort someone unless you cry with them. I think big brother Kenneth cried, too, but he wouldn't say so. He did a real religious thing all of a sudden. He crawled out from under the table and told Pat and me that we should do the same. His idea was to go over to the window where we could look out over the west eighty acre line and the tree line. This would be the last hill the folks would have to pass over before they got home. By the way, Alice and I just stopped by to look at the old home place as we came from South Dakota. The west eighty looked the same as it did half a century ago.

Kenny's command was: "If we really pray, the Lord will send the folks home." I think Pat and I could have prayed just as well under the table, but not with big brother in command. We knelt down in a straight row, side by side, with Pat in the middle and right in front of the window. We cried, we prayed, but nothing happened. It's an awful thing to pray and not receive an answer; especially when your sister is crying for the folks and she's scared. I remember the lightning flashed all of a sudden. The clap of thunder really shook the frame part of our house. You can't blame Pat for running back and crawling under the table. Shame on any boy who would leave his sister all alone when she was frightened. It was my brotherly duty so I got real close to her under the table again, and so did my brother Kenny. Pat cried and I cried to comfort her.

Then Kenneth got real religious again. He crawled back out from under the table and said, "We got to do it all over again. We didn't do it right. The Sunday School teacher said you have to have faith when you pray or it won't do any good to pray." He had us kneel down again and right in front of the window, facing the west eighty. First Kenny, then Pat, and then me. I don't know where he got the idea, but he said, "I'm going over to the cook stove and get a match." He did and then said, "I'm going to light it and let it burn. We are going to pray and believe God. He'll send the folks over the hill." I can still see that match burning. We watched and we prayed. We looked at the west eighty. We really were praying. The match burned shorter and shorter. It almost burned out, when the lights of the Model T shot up over the west eighty hill. I don't remember what happened to the storm; I am still amazed; I am still thrilled. I learned one of the dearest lessons of my life. If you believe God; if you have real faith, God will answer prayer.

2
Childhood Memories Continued

Sister Florence (Pat) and William 3 Years Old

The previous chapter was written for the Gale Family Reunion. A few memories were meant just for the family and I perhaps should have omitted them. It does take you into my boyhood. Other happenings of my childhood I wish to include in Chapter Two. These occurred mainly in Wyoming and Colorado.

This was a time remembered as the "dust bowl years" in the late 1920's and most of the 1930's. One encyclopedia dates the "Great Depression" as 1929-1941. It did not cover quite all the United States. It did affect all of the states and the whole world in general.

12 million men were out of work. Freight trains were loaded with men from all over the country who rode the rails. We lived near the main line of the Union Pacific Railroad. Men were riding on and in boxcars and coal cars. Some just hung to the ladders of the train cars. These men would tell one another where people lived who would serve them meals. They referred to themselves as bums. Actually, most were good men hunting for work.

Many came to the boxcar where we lived. Often they wanted to work for their meals. Dad and Mom bought beans by the 100 pound bags. Mother fed them beans and cornbread.

There were many months in Colorado and Nebraska when our furniture collected red dust blowing from Oklahoma. The sky looked dusty with a reddish color. We traveled when the dust was so thick that the car headlights could not be seen. Someone would stand on the fenders to help the driver keep on the road.

There were fences that became completely covered with drifting sand. In other places the sand moved from the wind blowouts until it cut new gulches and left the fences and posts hanging in the air.

Grasshoppers were so thick they looked like clouds. They ate the vegetation the drought had not destroyed. Families burned fields of corn for lack of market value. See Happy Happenings (THE PONY BROUGHT US HOME). This is a memory from the Dust Bowl Depression. Someone wrote a song called "It Ain't Gonna Rain No More."

Mr. Garven owned a store in Berthound, Colorado. He gave us credit for groceries. He told the customers, "We go through this together." When we moved away we owed a big grocery bill. He never pressured us to pay. It was many months, even a few years before mother could say, "I am finally paying the last of our grocery bill." She tried to pay at least a small amount every month. We three older children gave all we could earn to help keep food on the table.

Many of us children felt we were the only ones affected by the drought and depression. We lived to learn how our nation was affected. Under President Franklin Roosevelt, the government initiated work projects called WPA (Work Progress Administration) and CCC (Civilian Conservation Corps). Young men were employed in the latter program to work on conservation projects. These programs provided work for many men. Tree belts were planted and many construction projects were accomplished. Folks worked for what they got. For the very needy who could not work, federal money was provided by grants.

We lived on a big ranch where my father was foreman. Many things happened that I'll not forget. Rattlesnakes became dangerous on the prairies. One day my brother Kenneth and I were walking down a plowed furrow. Kenneth was in the lead carrying a .22 rifle. We both heard a rattlesnake buzz. You never forget the sound after you hear it a few times. My brother made a jump from the furrow. I felt a yank on the back of my pant leg. I looked back to see the rattler that struck. It was coiling up. I tried to tell Kenneth where it was. He shot and said, "I got it." I said, "No, you didn't." He pulled up the rifle and shot again. He claimed he got it. I could tell the one that struck me was still alive because of the buzzing. Kenneth stepped over and shot again. Three rattlers all within 10 feet of each other. He shot them all in the head. He did brag about being a good shot. I think he was. Someone told us that rattlesnakes line their heads so they look down the barrel of a gun.

There was a prairie dog town in the pasture on our place. I think the prairie dogs, owls and rattlesnakes all live in the same holes. About three blocks from our house I saw a big rattler crawling. I ran up to try to kill it with my hoe. It got into a yucca plant. (We called them soap weeds). I was poking around trying to get it to crawl out. When I looked up, it was about a foot above the soap weed. It was near striking distance of me. It frightened me so that I threw the hoe at it. The blade caught it a few inches below its head. The force of the hoe pulled the snake nearly out of the soap weed. I got my hoe and finished cutting the head off. It was so long and heavy that I dragged it home and put it in the barn.

The next day I took Kenneth out to show him. I was ahead of him when he grabbed my arm and pulled me back. He yelled, "There's a snake in there!" I replied, "Well, that's what I'm going to show you." He said, "This one is alive; I heard it buzz." An empty barrel was sitting on the edge of a two-inch board. Kenneth knocked it over. A big Western Diamondback like the one I killed was coiled and buzzing. When we got it killed, we found it had a rattle with 14 joints and a button on its tail.

The one I had killed had 11 joints and a button. It looked as if a few had been broken off. They claim rattlers gain one joint each year. These were the biggest snakes we ever killed. What Kenneth and I concluded was that I had dragged and made a trail that the rattler's mate could follow. A cowboy gave a good price for them. He skinned them and glued the skins on saddles.

I do have several other snake stories, but I'll just share one more. My sister Pat and I were gathering wild flowers. I saw a velvet-type plant and asked Pat if she would like to use some stems from it for her bouquet. She said she would. When I stood up, I had a small prairie rattler wrapped up in the plant. I held it about in the middle. I both felt and heard the buzz. I dropped it mighty quick and killed it with a rock as it started to crawl away.

Out on those Colorado prairies they had county rodeos that were geared to all ages. I learned to ride steers with a cirsingle, a rope with a loop on one end which is wrapped around the steer's belly and back through the loop. The rider holds the rope tight with one hand. As the steer bucks out of the chute, the event is timed.

One year I rode a steer until the shot of the gun and won first prize. The shot frightened the steer and he ran right between the cowboys on horses and out into the open. I was afraid of being trampled by the horses. The steer ran full speed. When I finally jumped off, I landed in a big bed of cacti. I rolled in it and got needles all over me. The cowboys took me back to where my pony was and used pliers to pull the needles. I had to lead my pony home; I hurt too bad to ride. Mother Nature and time worked wonders in healing me up for another adventure.

There was one account from the Nebraska Sandhills that I think you would enjoy. The school we attended required a 3.5 mile horseback ride. Mother bought Kenneth and me each a couple pair of coveralls. These were cheaper than shirts and pants. They had a button-type end gate on the backside. So did my long legged underwear. One day when I went to the outside school toilet, I got some of the underwear and coverall mixed up when I was buttoning them. The girls laughed and teased me. I must have looked funny. I have disliked coveralls ever since.

An enjoyable incident happened when one of the boys was returning from the outside toilet. He saw an airplane about to fly over the school house. He ran to the door and yelled "Airplane." We had recess right then. We boys went out the windows; the girls crowded through the door. For days we talked about the first airplane we had ever seen.

My Aunt Bessie told us about the first car that came through our area. The people lined the road. When it was nearing the time for the car to come, two horseback riders came ahead. They told everyone to stand back, "The car will pass this point at 20 miles an hour; that is a dangerous speed." Aunt Bessie, listening to the conversation heard a man say they were building a car that would go 30 miles an hour. Somebody laughed and said, "They can't do that; you couldn't breathe at that speed."

Those were the "good old days!" The roads in our area were car tracks. When you met a car, you were to pull over and use just one track. The other car pulled over and used the other one. Generally it would be a neighbor, so you would stop and visit a while. One neighbor said to my Dad, "Bill, you folks haven't been to our place for a long time. Why don't you come over for dinner?" Dad and Mom decided to postpone our trip to North Platte and went home with them for a meal. The women cooked; the men talked; we children played. It would be something if we could slow down to that pace again.

One of our worst wrongs was when watermelons were ripe. The different neighbors got into our patch and we got into theirs. We sometimes ate them together. We thought of it as sport and even bragged about doing it. When I got saved, I had to make some restitutions that took the sport out of it.

Neighbors came to my father when they needed help regarding their horses and cattle. Dad would look at the horse's teeth and tell its age. He watched them walk to determine if they had strained muscles or other problems. He seemed to know what to do about ranching and farming problems.

My father explained that horses' shoulders could be sweenied (meaning wasted in different ways). When cowboys rope wild horses, large bulls or steers, it is very important that the saddle horse be facing the roped animal. A sideways sudden yank or pull could dislocate the horse's muscles and ruin it for roping. The large work horse that likes to pull can easily be hurt if it has a cross-pull against the shoulders. Both of these situations could cause a sweeny and destroy the horse's usefulness. My father could recognize this problem by the way saddle horses or draft horses walked.

We had two horses that we rode to school. My Uncle Doc claimed Lady and Uncle Tom claimed Buck. Lady was a small-built, gentle mare, brown in color. Buck was a big, raw-boned buckskin gelding. He was frisky and loved to run. He was the fastest of all the riding ponies at our school. Dad made us take good care of these two horses. We had to keep them curried and fed.

My father, Bill Gale, was second in command over the city park at North Platte, Nebraska for many years. The world champion horse shoe player and his wife came to the park. I saw her throw a horse shoe and knock an apple off her husband's head and make a ringer. He played a game with my father and beat him by seventeen points. He said, "I'll give you that many points and we'll play again." I was a little kid looking on. The park crew went home for dinner. Dad ate his lunch and then played horse shoe with the world's champion. The park crew didn't know about the extra points. They arrived in time to see Dad beat the world champion. He said to Dad, "Bill, don't tell them about the extra points." Those men really bragged on Dad. He just laughed and said, "I had to play hard to beat him."

My mind races when I think of my boyhood. My friend Virgil and I attended the Nazarene Sunday School. Virgil was promoted to an older class. He was about six months older than I. We both dropped out because we wanted to be in class together. After we missed a few times, the staff became lenient and advanced me into Virgil's class. We were happy again. Lenore Ball was our teacher. She taught by asking questions about the lesson. My first Sunday to be back in Sunday School, she asked one question that no one could answer. I was the last one to be asked and was able to give the right answer.

After class, she motioned me up to her desk. She said she was proud of me for answering the hard question. Then she said, "I want you here every Sunday to help with the difficult questions." I had to really study the lesson. Those other dumb kids wouldn't be able to answer some of her questions. I still remember that she put her arm around me when she said she was proud of me. I didn't dare let her down. There are many kids out there that would respond to a little kindness and a loving smile. I always wanted to be good. I excelled more in pranks. I liked to have others laugh with me. Lots of things I did as pranks, I would go and fix up later.

Mother, having been a school teacher, was the neighborhood mathematician. Men measured their stacks of hay for length and width by running their tapes over the top and down to the ground. She took those measurements and soon told them how many ton of hay were in the stacks.

As far back as I can remember, whether in the old sod house or the boxcar home, we had lots of neighborhood people (elementary, high school, and college students) come to our home in the evenings. Sometimes they would come late at night to have Mother help them with their school work. She would end up by giving readings to us. She knew hundreds of them from memory.

Late in her life Mother told me that she didn't think I ever went to the pulpit to preach but what she went to her knees. She meant that she prayed for me. I miss my mother. She was a childhood memory and a lifetime memory as well.

One day, my cousin and I were walking down 7th Street next to the railroad tracks. We were skipping rocks to see who could make the longest skip and also who could make a rock skip the most times. A man driving a new shiny car came down the street. My cousin said, "Let's see if we can skip a stone under the car." We threw at the same time. One stone made it, but one banged up under the car. I doubt if it damaged the car, but it did anger the driver. He made a fast turn around in the street and took after us. We ran across lots, zig-zagged up alleys and down streets. He jumped curbs and drove as fast as he could. As he drove around the blocks, his tires screeched. I feel certain he would have run over us if he could have. When he turned to go around one more block, we came out behind him. He must not have seen us in his mirrors.

It was prayer meeting night at the Nazarene Church. I never ran so far and hard to go to church. We sat down quickly and started worshiping. I mean we both watched and prayed. The church folk welcomed us. This was our first prayer meeting to attend. Some one asked, "Why did you boys come tonight?" We assured them that we felt like we wanted to come and pray. After I was 21, I ran the mile in five minutes. I had gotten some training that night. It was a turning point in my life.

3
Meet My Family

Back Row: Alice E., Donald, and David
Front Row: William, Aleta, and Alice K.

y father was a great teacher. The following made memories: A one-legged milk stool; a barbed wire fence making a corral; many kinds of milk cows; my dad saying, "If a boy goes to school next year, he should know how to milk." I can't remember the names of the cows, but each was named for some lady. It was a job to learn to sit on a one-legged milk stool. Dad would say, "This cow is gentle. She has four teats. Now, take hold of the closest teats with your hands. Now squeeze and pull a little. That's it! Keep it up until all four are dry." It wasn't long until I was making lots of foam in the pail. Dad bragged on me. That made me feel big and important.

We were fixing fence out in the pasture. "Look here, Son." He told me there were three pedals on the Model T Ford: one clutch, one brake and the middle one reverse. I was a big nine-year-old lad. "Watch me, boy! Forward; stop; backward! Now see if you can do it. Say, that's great." I had already practiced a lot with the car sitting still. He taught me how to shift it into high. I learned to drive in the pasture and helped Dad fix fence, drive staples, stretch wire and then drive the car up a ways.

I can still hear Dad say, "Lady is a gentle horse. Take her bridle reins; lead her over by the bank; now grab her mane and crawl on. Now you're a cowboy, ride hard." "Thanks, Dad." I went on to learn to ride even when they bucked. I could rope calves for branding.

"Son, I want you to drive this big truck. For the first lesson, ride with me and watch me. On this big hill, you have to shift down. Watch me double clutch. Now, remember the same gear it takes to climb the hill will be safe to use when going down. When it is dark and the car ahead is going so slow that you need to pass, remember this: Go out far enough to get back if you need to. If the approaching car lights look like one light, there is enough room to pass. If you see two head lights, don't try to pass. It is too close."

My Dad taught me how to plumb when they stomped oakum (a stringy fiber). This was used for pouring melted babbitt for cast iron sewer lines. He taught me how to read a framing square to lay out buildings and to cut rafters.

He taught me to tip my hat when proper and to take it off when talking to ladies. He taught me to speak to my aunts and uncles using those titles. I was to address adults as Mr. and Mrs.

When I told him the Lord had called me to preach, he said, "I want you to be a good one." He sold his car and bought me a 1928 Model A Ford. He walked back and forth to work (over two miles one way) so I could have a car for my ministry.

One day, my father came home drunk when I was a little lad. Mother cried and said, "Daddy, why did you do it? Our relatives are coming for supper." He said, "I'll go walk it off." He took me by the hand and we walked out into the pasture. He stopped to vomit on the way. He finally sobered up and had me sit beside him. He told me to never drink that rotten stuff, for it would ruin me. I promised I never would. I tried it a couple of times and made a fool out of myself. I remembered his warning. He said he could take a social drink and then leave it alone, but it got the best of him. I never saw him sober for several years. Our home was broken. Mother lived with my family for many years. She loved Dad and he loved her, but drink ruined our home. My brother Bud cared for Dad for many years.

Mother's prayers and Bud's care are the big reason my father, my teacher and my hero got saved. I often talked to Dad and prayed with him. He did say, "Son, I hope to get saved some day and when I do, I want the kind of religion you have."

After I left home at 15, I never came home to live. I tried to make annual visits. I held a few revival meetings in my hometown of North Platte, Nebraska. On one of those trips, I stopped at my brother Alfred's home. He had a bunch of Western books to take to Dad. He told me he was going so I went with him. Dad was sitting in a soft chair in the rest home. We greeted and Alfred gave him the books. I said, "That's a lot of reading. If you told me you were reading the Bible, it would sure make my day." He said, "Reach up on the shelf. I am reading the Bible through. It is open to the place where I am reading." He had read over half way through the Bible. It made my day. I said, "Dad, if you told me you got saved it would make my trip." He took over to say, "Duane (often he called me by my middle name since both of our first names are William), I was sitting here just as I am now. I looked over by the cot where I sleep. There sat several empty whiskey bottles. One "fifth" had a little left in it. I thought I better kill it." Dad said, "When I got up, I said out loud, 'Bill Gale, you old fool, that is the way they will find you one of these days. You will be dead with a bunch of empty liquor bottles lying there to show what did it.'"

He went on to say, "I went over and fell on my knees and laid over on my bed. I told the Lord, 'My boy William told me that when I came to the end and didn't know what to do, I should turn to Jesus. He would be there to save me.'" Dad continued, "I cried and He saved me and from that day to this I have never had a desire to drink." That did make my trip.

Sometime later we were all at my sister Pat and Glen Jergensen's home. We were having a good time talking together as siblings. I looked over and there on the love seat were Mother and Father. They were back in one another's love. I said to our group, "We'll never see a more beautiful sight. That proves Calvary's atonement is still working."

As he neared death from a heart attack a few months later, he told the family he was ready to meet the Lord. He then asked, "Where is Mom?" They told him someone had gone to get her. Heaven has taken on a brighter look since Dad is there.

Mother, Cynthia Chamberlain Gale, was a loved marvel. I have already written much about her. She came to live with our family after Mother and Dad separated. She had her strengths and her weaknesses. We learned to endure her being a "second mother" in the home and enjoyed her love for the Lord and for all of us.

During her Normal (Teacher's) Training, she excelled in mathematics. Algebra, geometry, trigonometry and calculus were all a challenge to her. There likely were not many subjects she did not enjoy. She seemed to memorize more easily than the average person. Memorization was a natural part of her life. As a lad, I learned to go to sleep with her scripture quotations and her readings. Since I have two poems I wish to include, I'll limit pages which I could write about Mother. (See Chapter IV).

Mother, Aunt Bessie, and Aunt Lena, all were pleasant persons. We children: cousins, nieces and nephews, were always excited to be with them. I have three full tapes of Mother's readings. A large portion of a notebook contains her readings. When she was in her 90's she recited from memory "You Tell Me I Am Growing Old" with strong feeling. She perhaps had the most requests for "Stretch the Table Out."

My wife Alice and I were in the Philippines when Mother died. I wrote a letter in advance and asked our son David to read it at her funeral. We had gone to see Mother before we went overseas. When I took her in my arms to tell her goodbye, we wept together. I told her to find Dad and we'll try to come through the Eastern Gate. We plan to see our loved ones there.

My brother, Kenneth Austin, eldest of the eight Gale children, was wonderfully saved from drink. He was great in sports and my boyhood hero.

Sister Florence Marie (we called her Pat) loaned me her typewriter for a year and sent spending money to me when I went away to Bible School. She was my best chum.

Darrell was the brother just younger than I. He was a very good mechanic, but drink became his downfall. I felt such a prayer burden that I told my wife I needed to go to North Platte to see him. We stopped first at my sister Pat's home. She came to where we were as we got out of the car. I said, "We stopped by to tell you we had arrived. We are going to see Mom and Dad first." Pat said, "Wait, my phone is ringing." When she returned, she told us that Darrell had died just as they got him to the hospital. We had made the trip mainly to pray with him. I was in a state of shock.

I leaned over his casket and whispered, "Darrell, I came all this way to pray with you to help you get ready for death. You died just before I got to see you. I can't understand why it happened so close to my coming." Never had a sweeter peace come to me as it did when looking into my brother's face. It seemed the Lord came. I could feel His presence and was impressed that I would see Darrell again. I left the casket assured that the Lord had spoken to me.

I told Frank, his son, that I was going to the police station. I wanted to talk to the men who had picked Darrell up. Frank said, "Let's go together, I need to get his clothes."

The officer said, "We have picked Darrell up several times when he was drinking, but this time there was no alcohol in his blood. He said he was not drinking, but needed to be taken to the hospital."

My cousin Bonnie was at the hospital when we stopped there. She said, "William, Darrell told me when they were helping him into the emergency room that he was hurting in his chest." He was sober with no sign of drink.

A few days later, Mother got a letter from a pastor in McCook, Nebraska. He had learned of Darrell's death. He wrote that Darrell had been saved in one of their services. He told the pastor of his drink problem and the pastor had him stay at their home for days. My brother told the minister that he was "dried out." In the letter the pastor reported that Darrell had a good testimony the morning of the day he died.

All the facts put together made me understand. I was glad Mother let me read the letter. She lost it and couldn't remember the church or the pastor's name. I couldn't remember either. I have not been brief in this section, but I wanted all of the family to know about Darrell.

My brother Calvin and wife Vada gave many years to Indian ministry, pastoring the Wesleyan Indian Missions Church at Lake Andes, South Dakota. The Native people met for a service and gave Calvin an Indian name which means, "The Man Who Loves Everybody."

Brother Alfred worked for the Union Pacific Railroad for many years. His wife Virginia is a great cook. Both like to fish. They have canned food for us for a long time. We seldom eat a meal but what part of it came from them.

Sister Ruth Kalb is a nurse and a missionary. She and her husband Albert spent two terms in Sierra Leone, Africa and several years with a missionary group called "The Sowers." Their lives have been devoted to missions.

Joel David (Bud) is the youngest of the eight Bill Gale brood. He and his wife Delores (Tootie) live in North Platte, Nebraska where he has been a fireman for 37 years. In a recent year, he was honored as "Fire Captain" and received "Employee of the Year Award." He was chosen by vote of members of the Fire Department.

4

Tell It with Poetry

Mother Cynthia Gale

MEET MY FAMILY continues with a collection of poems I wrote for family gatherings. Several were written with no thought of making copies. While traveling in the interest of the Indian Work, I wrote poetry to spice up my presentations.

Being a 4th generation Gale boy limits my ability to trace our family history. However, I understand that Great Grandfather Gale's first name was William. If you find that I am wrong, please don't tell me. Someone suggested that he came to this country as an immigrant from Ireland and that he was adopted into a family by the name of Gale. His loving wife came from good Irish stock as her name was Kelly. The Kellys are a big part of our family. My grandfather, John Baker Gale, married into the Britt family. His first wife Sarah, was the mother of Grace. After Sarah's decease, Grandfather Gale married her sister Chloe Irene Britt. She had four girls and five boys making it a family of five girls and five boys.

Mother's most recited poem:

STRETCH THE TABLE OUT

It was not too much work for her in the days of long ago
To get a dinner ready for a dozen friends or so,
My mother never grumbled at the cooking she must do
Or the sweeping or the dusting but she seemed to smile it through
And the times that we were happiest beyond the slightest doubt
Was when good friends were coming and she stretched the table out.

We never thought when we were young to take our friends away
And entertain them at a club or a swell café
When my mother gave a dinner she planned it all herself
And fed the people that she liked the best things on the shelf.
The one task always came to me for I was young and stout
I brought the leaves to Father when he stretched the table out.

That queer, old-fashioned table, I can see it yet today
With its curious legs of finished oak, round which I used to play
It wasn't much to look at, not as handsome or refined
Or as costly or as splendid as the modern oval kind
But it always had a welcome for our friends to sit about
And though twenty guests were coming we could always stretch it out.

I learned it from Mother – it is foolish pride to roam
The only place to entertain your friends is right at home.
Then bring them in dozens, let them laugh and sing and play,
And learn to love and know them in the good old-fashioned way.
Home's the place for fun and frolic. Home's the place where joys may
    sprout,
And if you crowd our dining room, we'll just stretch the table out.

Some day we'll leave this earthly home and journey to the sky.
Some day the silver cord will break and we will say good-bye.
But when we get to heaven, that good old-fashioned home
We'll hang our hats upon the rack, at last we'll cease to roam.
And then our blessed Lord will say when He hears our joyous shout,
Hurry, angels, saints are coming, "Let us stretch the table out."

—Anonymous

YOU TELL ME I AM GETTING OLD

You tell me I am getting old
I tell you that's not so!
The "House" I live in is worn out
And that, of course, I know.

It's been in use a long, long while;
It's weathered many a gale;
I'm really not surprised you think it's
Getting somewhat frail.

The color is changing on the roof,
The window is getting dim,
The wall's a bit transparent and
Looking rather thin.

The foundation not so steady as
Once it used to be –
My "house" is getting shaky, but my
"House" isn't ME!

My few short years can't make me old.
I feel I'm in my youth.
Eternity lies just ahead, a life of
Joy and truth.

I'm going to live forever, there;
Life will go on – it's grand!
You tell me I am getting old?
I just don't understand.

The dweller of my little "House"
Is young and bright and gay;
Just starting on a life to last
Throughout eternal day.

You only see the outside, which is
All that most folks see
You tell me I am getting old?
You mixed my house with ME!

      —Anonymous
   Mother's personal testimony in her later years.

My Queen

Words here written are not for show,
Of a wonderful person you should know
It all began in nineteen twenty and four
When the stork flew in the Jones' front door.

The first delivered that early fall,
A girl so sweet, angelic and small.
Free from envy and from malice
The tacked on title named her Alice.

Vern, Dave, Don, and Ralph young misters
With Edith, Irene and Lavonne for sisters.
Father a Welsh mister, and Mother a Swede
A great combination, yes, indeed.

Parents and children all so kind
A finer family it is hard to find.
Her added squeal broke the slumber,
Third of the brood was her number.

We've mentioned the family, so on with the tale
Describing this darling, words nearly fail.
It was something new upon the farm
So full of love and full of charm.

Energy plus, and excelling joy,
Oft times wished she were a boy.
Driving truck or tractor, happy she
Out of doors life was her glee.

One of her tricks was not so nice
For in her pocket she carried mice.
Since they were dead, and round and fat,
She carried them home to feed her cat.

The words flow forth with ready ease
But not intended to merely tease.
This account is not just rumor
Nor penned alone for laugh and humor.

Sorting mavericks is a battle.
How she thrilled to round up cattle.
She looked to be a delicate lass,
As Herefords munched upon the grass.

Fearful of water, boat and paddle
While right at home in the saddle.
Little school house round the turn
It was easy for her to learn.

Tomboy acts are rather shady,
She changed her ways to a perfect lady.
To teach others the good old rule
She spent much time teaching school.

As a teacher, good, you may ask?
She gave herself to her task.
Math, and history, or just plain grammar,
For some thick skulls you need a hammer.

Cooking, baking is the life
Wooed him sweetly, became his wife
This to her was a new role
From the very moment the bell did toll.

No longer now was she a teacher
Delightful new job, manage a preacher.
Fiery sermons, acceptable arson
"Preach it hot," she urged her parson.

Life dedicated fully to another,
Children four, a loving mother.
Rather slight is her size
Yet she surely deserves a prize.

Pin gently on her a fragrant Petal,
Right beside it a Golden Medal.
Set her now in royal scene,
A humble tribute, she is my Queen.

William D. Gale

This poem was written some time after Alice Kathryn and I were married. The Joneses so kindly welcomed me into the family.

SON DAVID GALE

Yes, it is golden; it is fifty
And a great half century
A time for celebration
On this anniversary

How well do I remember
When you made your first big squeal
We welcomed you our first born
And your life became so real

When you were yet in your cradle
When you started out to tease
Though in your boyish fashion
You always tried to please

How proud we were of our boy
When you started out to school
Your conduct and report card
Proved you lived the golden rule

First your high school diploma
With honors you had earned
And next your Bachelor's Degree
As a man you now have turned

Vermillion, South Dakota
Conferred a Master's Degree
How happy were us parents
And as proud as we could be

'Twas a great big occasion
When you at Iowa State
Were awarded PHD
An honor that was first rate

The big event now followed
When wedding bells rang loud
Elizabeth now your bride
With a joyful, happy crowd

What a wond'rous happening
When sweet Heather came to stay
A welcomed bundle of love
Now to brighten every day

Your quiver was made clear full
By Michael a bouncing boy
This bundle of excitement
Has so filled your home with joy

David, you're our champion
These few words are a token
Of a love bond deeply felt
That can never be broken

David is our eldest. His scholarship was recognized through elementary, high school, and college. He has earned Bachelor's, Master's, and Doctoral degrees. He has also been awarded many local, state and national honors. David turned 50 in 1993 and is now a distinguished, white-haired senior.

ALICE ELIZABETH GALE CHURCHILL
50 YEARS

Let's ring the bells and ring them loud
Sound the bugle from off the cloud
What is the reason for this day?
To let her father have his say

She's far more precious than a pearl
The grandest gift – our baby girl
So now the sun would always shine
Into our hearts love to entwine

What a darling sweetheart lass
Her arrival was just first class
Not with fanfare or not with show
Just by her coming made it so

Alice Elizabeth her name
It was chosen before she came
February 9 was the date
Arrived on time, loving sedate

Her childhood passed with rapid pace
This one made for ribbons and lace
Gained her height by time she was ten
Can't explain it now, even then

Children services all done right
Her stories were children's delight
Anointing came down from above
It was accented by her love

When in college she met her flame
Mrs. Don Churchill she became
With much time in the parsonage
As a pastor's wife with her sage

Life not full with an empty nest
Mechele La Don brought that to rest
Our first grandchild a baby girl
It changed us so with raptured thrill

Next big Donald made himself known
On arrival he looked half grown
Proud parents – a girl and boy
Filling our lives with wondrous joy

Sis, your life full of interest took
Enough to fill a great big book
Golden age – it just can't be true
The half century mark has caught you

You have been faithful through this span
Earned the respect of fam'ly clan
Your love for Jesus Christ our Lord
Adds reason why you are adored

And now you're a senior, you know
One of the queens – heading the show
We proud parents bow in salute
To pen these lines in our tribute

Alice is a busy, talented lady: working with children, wonderful home decorator, a lovable person with oceans of friends. She reached the 50 mark in 1995. We would not trade her for all the fish in the ocean.

MY SON DONALD

It seems now a yesterday, my lad
When you were a babe, my pride and joy
Rollic and frolic in trundle bed
The passing years have so quickly sped

Quickly you've grown to be a man
And answered the call from Uncle Sam
It seems as if your life just begun
And now how I miss you so, my son

If the years I myself could undo
I would plan more time to be with you
Time for you my dear youngest lad
To be a more understanding Dad

Cherished memories of you are mine
Proud I am of a boy so fine
Protecting our land you have a heart
Gallant and bravely you'll do your part

In weeks ahead as you march and train
Be strong with courage to stand the strain
Stand by the right whatever the loss
Be a soldier for Christ of the cross

Remember son, whether far or near
Your earthly father feels you are dear
To the sov'reign Father you are one
Be loyal to Him you are His son

While "Old Glory" still waves o'er our land
Be true to her colors, firmly stand
Triumph will come engage in the strife
Your sacred trust may cost you your life

Don, my dear boy, whatever your care
Take time for the Bible and for prayer
First for your Maker the life you own
True values then to your country shown

If I could be with you I'd not hide
Proudly stand with you right by your side
Since I cannot in your battles share
I will lift for you often in prayer

We'll watch the day when your task is done
And you can return safely to home
We'll hang the welcome mat on the door
Life will become normal as before

   Donald, our youngest son, was gifted in many ways and notably for
his special touch on the piano. He became a sergeant in the military. We
greatly miss him and his music. He passed away October 22, 1986.

ALETA BLUE: FIFTY

Fifty years of ribbon and lace
Our baby girl before our face
You joined the club; it cannot be
Now a member in jubilee

Golden the color marks the day
It's fifty full years so they say
Sage may count five decades to be
But still make it half century

Found us because your own dear Sis
Prayed for a sister; wouldn't miss
Two boys and girls, perfect number
A bigger house, lots of lumber

You came home one day as a lass
Saying, "Outran all the girls in your class"
Another of your classic joys
You'd beat all but one of the boys

The years have passed so rapidly
School days, marriage and your fam'ly
Justin Allen, athletic lad
Then Del William to make us glad

You worked so hard; seldom to roam
From it came a nice lovely home
Kept very neat like a king's room
So cozy with flowers in bloom

You faced a sadness; home broken
Your car wreck; near death spoken
Auto sales met sag in market
Queen of car sales was the target

These reverses enough to stop
Our plucky girl climbed on top
We are so proud of how you prayed
Defeated not; for right you stayed

A partner, true friend, Cindy came
She helped Aleta win the game
Sons stood with you; each a real man
And you rank high in the Gale Clan

With tribute and praise as before
You are the one we all adore
Single handed built a new home
Kitchen and house plan all your own

Know you're a Gale girl from the start
In each enterprise do your part
Proud of you, love you, you're our gal
And all through life a sweetheart pal.

Aleta, our youngest, reached her half century mark February 28, 2003. It seems impossible to her parents that our baby girl can be this age. She is a lady in business and sales and our pride and joy.

5

School Days

William with Friendly Collie

S chool days, school days
Oh, them golden rule days
Readin' and 'ritin', and 'rithmatic
Taught to the tune of the hickory stick.

You were my queen in calico
I was your barefoot, bashful beau
You wrote on my slate, "I love you so"
When we were a couple of kids.

Whittier School was a little white-frame building about 3.5 miles from our home in Lincoln County near to Stapleton, Nebraska. In 1926, I, William Duane, enrolled in first grade. I had red hair and a freckled face. It was 16 years later that I graduated from Tabor Bible School in Iowa. This was a period of discipline for me. What the Lord allowed to happen during those years is quite interesting.

We moved to Maxwell, Nebraska while I was still in primary grades. Our house there was located adjacent to the elementary and junior high school. We were affected by a sudden change. We would wait until the last minute (perhaps second) to start running toward the school. When they saw Kenneth, Pat, and me running, they would ring the bell a little longer so we wouldn't be late.

In the school building they actually had running water. When I saw the kind of toilets they had, I was scared nearly to death. I was afraid I couldn't flush them and was scared to try. I hoped I could hold out until recess and then I would run home to our outside toilet. That was wishful thinking. I lost the battle. The teacher finally came and stood by my desk. She said, "Class, I am letting all of you go out for recess." When the room cleared, she took her hand off my shoulder and said, "William, you have had an accident. You slip home and clean up and come back." I hurried out, but was ashamed to go home. I hid so I thought no one could see me. The teacher got my brother Kenneth and told him where I was hiding. She said he should get me to go home. He came roaring like a bulldozer and informed me I had messed my britches and the teacher had told him to take me home. I ran like greased lightning to get away from Kenneth. He ran fast to do his duty. There had been a hard rain that had formed a mud puddle about half a block wide. I ran out in the middle of it and dared Kenneth to come and get me. I said I would plaster him with mud.

He went home and told Mother. When he returned and headed toward the schoolhouse, he yelled, "Mom is going to get you." She waited a while and then gently came over to the fence and told me that water was not good on shoes. I said, "Yes, I know!" "Hurry home," she said, "and I'll help you clean up." My education was slowed down a bit, but, not altogether. I did learn how to flush a toilet. That's something that has been helpful all my life.

We moved from Maxwell, Nebraska to Wyoming and then on to Colorado. I got the whooping cough and missed 6 weeks of school. My teacher and my mother thought I should repeat the fourth grade. I was kind of dumb anyway and also had missed too many days of school. I spent two years in that grade, so it became my favorite. I turned out to be one of the smartest in the class! I even tried to help some who were dumber than I. This helped me catch up in my education.

Those were depression days. I got a job picking chickens in a poultry house on Saturdays and some other special days. After school, I washed dishes in a Greek restaurant until midnight. We three oldest: Pat, Kenneth, and I brought our checks home and put them into the grocery fund. We all had to work to earn a living. We had rent, fuel, medical, grocery and many other bills to pay. We could always get our clothing from the Salvation Army Thrift Store.

I don't think I was ever mean, but I pulled pranks to have fun. At school there were times when I was to be punished that I asked the teachers if I could go home early instead of staying after school. They let me work my own schedule.

Miss Post kept me after school until six o'clock one evening. She told me to copy a page out of an encyclopedia and then I could go. I showed her my handwriting after I had copied a little. I suggested that she would be able to read it better out of the reference book itself. She got tickled and I had lots of fun. It was dark when she let me go. I explained that I was surprised she liked me so much. I told her that since it was getting dark a man might get her. She was a spinster and I think she liked the idea. I walked her home and we became the best of friends. When teachers laughed with me, I liked them and tried to do favors for them.

When I was in the 8th grade, because of a feud between the coach and me, he told me not to suit up. My home-room team won the class tour-nament and we played the 8th grade first string. I was washing dishes in the Greek restaurant and got to the game late. It was almost half-time and my team was 11 points behind. Our coach called time-out. He said, "Boys, Gale is hitting; feed him. Gale, use your right hand side hook and push shots." We were just one point behind. I was near mid-court and had two men guarding me when they yelled from the bleachers, "Shoot!" I heaved the ball hard in the direction of the goal. It swished without touching the rim. The gun went off with the ball in the air. The team carried me off the floor on their shoulders. We beat by one point. What I lacked in the classroom, I made up for in sports. In those days, they jumped center after every basket. There were no three point shots. The scores were lower than when the ball is taken out at the ends.

My freshman year I played football as a right halfback. One game I remember well. We were playing on the home field and our team was 3 points behind. Time was running out. We had one yard and one goal to go for a touch down. The coach sent word for Gale to carry the ball. I fumbled the ball. The final gun went off and we lost the game. Believe me if I had any pride, it was all gone!

The school system moved Mr. Dexter from junior high to senior high to coach the freshman-sophomore team. He still carried a grudge toward me. I had hopes of making the team, but he told me again that he would not choose me. I made the Round Robin team, which basically was the second string under another coach. We beat the first team in practice games more times than they beat us. Mr. Dexter came to me and said, "Gale, we better bury the hatchet." He had disappointed me so many times that I refused to play for him. If I had made the first string for my senior year, I would likely have missed going to Bible School and would have missed the life of Christian service. What a loss that would have been to me!

It seems I excelled in the wrong way. When I was in junior high, Southern Rose hair dressing was a plus for all the fellows. It was real greasy. It held your hair down and made it shine. Some one gave me a bottle and I was very happy. My hair was shiny like my classmates. The barbers would ask, "Do you want a hair cut or an oil change?" I finally ran out of my Rose Hair dressing. I melted lard and it was about as good, but we ran out of lard. I couldn't find any substitute until I saw the words "Cod Liver Oil" on a bottle. It held my hair in place and was more shiny than lard. I bounded off to school.

My gym glass came just before my study period. Mother had found some shirts that had good collars and cuffs, but the shirts themselves were rather ragged. She found two long sleeve sweaters in my size that were excellent. They covered the ragged parts of the shirts. That worked out well until I had to change after gym class. I would wait until the others were gone up for study period and then I would change in a hurry. I would be late for study hall, but I could get by that way. I came to school with my first application of cod liver oil and sweater-shirt combination. After gym class and the boys had gone up to study hall, I hurried into my ragged shirt. One of the boys came back to get something he had forgotten. His words were, "Look at that ragged shirt. Ha! Ha!" I thought he would tell everybody in school. I got my sweater on and rushed to the study hall. I knew my face was flushed. I felt so hot. I heard someone say, "Pew! Pew! Pew! Who's dead?" Soon others were saying, "Pew! Pew! Who's dead?" I said it, too, "Pew! Pew! Who's dead?" My ragged shirt under my nice sweater felt awfully warm. I knew who was dead. There was a flume-type fire escape by the side door. The study hall monitor stepped out into the hall and I slid down the fire escape.

I hurried out of the school yard and near to our home by the Union Pacific Round House where they worked on steam engines. I knew where there was a man-hole with a lid cover. I crawled down in it and pulled the lid back in place. I stayed there over four hours until the four o'clock whistle blew. This was where I spent my time when I played hooky from school.

The next day I bragged about how much fun I had. By the way, Southern Rose Hair Dressing came back on the market for a few weeks in 2002. I bought a bottle for old time's sake. It's not for use, but I'll gladly show it to you.

I did get started playing hooky. One time the truant officer came to our boxcar home to tell my mother that I had been skipping school. I heard Mother tell him that a boy of hers wouldn't do a thing like that! She told him I was sick and at home. He insisted she make me get dressed and go to school with him. He told me the next time he had to take me, it likely would be to the reform school in Kearney, Nebraska. He perhaps was right, except for the fact that I got saved. I went to Tabor Bible School. Aunt Rachel said she would see me in a month if not sooner. She felt I would be dismissed from school by that time.

Years later, my sister Pat and I were walking down the street. I waved at a man across the street. He smiled and waved back with enthusiasm. Pat asked, "Who is that man?" "That's a man I used to go to school with," I answered. "He's a lot older than you," my sister said. My reply was, "I know that. He is the truant officer."

One time when I played hooky, a friend and I tried to catch a ride on the four o'clock freight train. I grabbed for the train car where the ladder extended all the way to the top. If I had caught it, the speed of the train would have caused me to wrap around the end of the boxcar. This would have twisted my hands loose and let me drop down on the rail. Many bums have been killed by the wheels cutting them to pieces. I did catch the front of the next car. It threw me up against the side of the car and I lost my grip. I landed in cinders and rolled clear down the embankment. The train slowed down some and I was able to catch another train car and ride safely into town. My friend had a safe arrival, also. I took time to thank God for His mercy in sparing my life. *SUNSHINE and SHADOWS* records a host of happenings. Many of these show how God gave me another chance.

In review of my life in public school, I think I wanted to be a winner. I did it in the boxing ring. I ran like a scared deer when I carried the football. When a long distance runner, I did well. We were poor; the firemen brought us toys at Christmas time. We dressed from the Salvation Army Thrift Store. The boxcar home almost shouted, "Poor people live here." I had to learn from II Corinthians 8:9, "For ye know the grace of our Lord Jesus Christ, that, though he be rich, yet for your sakes he became poor, that ye through his poverty might be rich."

Through Jesus and redemption, we all became equal. In a church I attended, they were singing, "A tent or a cottage, why should I care? They're building a mansion for me over there." I have lived in a tent and a boxcar, so I had them sing, "A tent or a boxcar, why should I care?"

Though I have not always been in public or private schools, I have always been in God's school. I have been a dull scholar, but God seems to love the poor and needy. I am glad I found the Nazarene Church and learned how I could be saved and Tabor Bible School so I could learn how to keep saved.

6
Bible School Days

Brother Calvin and William with His First Car – 1928 Model A Ford

everend L.M. Rambo, pastor of the First Nazarene Church at North Platte, Nebraska, came to our home for a visit. He was a short, white-haired man who was loved by all the church people. I was especially fond of him. He was very kind to me and overlooked my faults.

On this occasion, I thought I would have a little fun so I said, "Rev. Rambo, I would like to go to Bible School and I need you to write a recommendation for me." I sort of laughed. I knew he would remember some of my pranks. One service I sat near the front of the church and whenever someone looked at me, I would yawn. Nearly the whole church got to yawning.

During one midweek prayer meeting, some of us boys rolled pastor's car up against the front door. Then we rolled the car belonging to the Sunday School Superintendent against the back door of the small bungalow-type building. The congregation couldn't get out so they helped a little fat boy through the window. They finally put three or four more children out to help push the cars away. We were nearby in case of emergency. I knew Pastor Rambo was suspicious of my being in on the act. I was certain he wouldn't want to write a recommendation. He was a wise pastor. He said, "Let's go out to my car and talk about it." He was very kind and said he would write the letter. As a result, I was accepted at Tabor Bible School in Iowa. The fun time with my pastor was a means of getting me headed in the right direction.

Mrs. Staples had a daughter named Mildred who attended Tabor. Her son Melvin had a train ticket he was not using and gave it to me. So Mildred and I traveled by train to school. This was my first experience at riding a passenger train.

The list of Bible School rules presented a challenge for me. The leaders, staff and students were very friendly but didn't appreciate my slang expressions. I told one of the teachers if she would make a list of good words, I would practice using them. If enough sandpaper is used, the rough places will be worn off. I think that is what happened to me.

At the school there was much hard manual labor to do besides mental work. I was put in charge of the dairy herd. This was before the days of milking machines. Most of the students got 10 cents an hour. I got the same, but was soon advanced to 14 cents. I know that sounds very low, but even grown men were receiving only $1.00 for a day's work. Our room and board was so reasonable that we could work off our school bill if we were good workers. I was soon running the printing presses as well as doing the cow chores. They advanced me to 17 cents an hour. During corn picking time in addition to these jobs, I was given the chore of shucking corn. They had a team of horses ready for me. I would shuck from 24 to 30 bushel, scoop it into the corn bins and make it to school by 9 o'clock. I would run the presses until midnight. To keep things livened up, I would pull some kind of prank. This got me into trouble occasionally. Some of us put tin cans on the bell clappers. Once we took a wagon apart and put it back together on top of a low-built silo. We put a horse's harness on a milk cow and tied her in the pastor's yard. Those things created some laughs. When I got saved, I became so busy holding street meetings, services in county homes, jails and rest homes that I didn't take time for pranks.

Courtship was a prohibited part of school life. I was a high school senior when Mary Alice Ward came to Tabor. I remarked to Daniel Page, "Do you see that pretty, black-haired girl going down the sidewalk? That's the girl for me!" He said, "As homely as you are, William, she'll never look your direction." For three years we had a smile for each other. The chapel room was also a study hall. Mary Alice sat three rows back of me. A picture up front served as a mirror. Occasionally we smiled at each other through the picture. When we came to chapel one morning, the principal said, "Some young folks have been flirting by way of the picture up front. We are having a few of you change seats." They had Mary Alice move up to where I was sitting and had me change with a young lady across the chapel who took Mary Alice's seat. I whispered, "Can you guess who has been flirting?" If that was what it was, I think it was stronger than that. This was a part of our courtship. Though Tabor Bible School had strict rules and standards, the leaders, teachers, printing staff and maintenance crew were some of the most dedicated and godly persons I have ever known. My life has been transformed by my association with them.

Bruce Mitchell taught me to run small hand printing presses and large paper presses. I learned to set up large and small frames of type. I made headings for articles from several different fonts of type. This exposure enabled me to gain knowledge in many areas of the printing business. I ran presses for printing *John Three Sixteen* and also *Good Tidings*, the official periodical of the Hephzibah Faith Missionary Association.

After I prayed through and got settled spiritually, the students voted for me to be president of the student body. It was about that time that I was called before the staff. The chairman said, "William, we are confused as to how to talk to you. Before you were saved, we were all happy for the way you worked. It was hard for us to decide to send you home. Now, that you are saved, you still have us worked up. We have made a list of eight jobs you are doing above your regular work load. You are to choose four from this list and give up the rest. Here is the list:"

1.   President of the student body (Like a youth pastor)

2.   Teacher – Boy's Sunday School Class

3.   President of Senior Class

4.   Pastor at Sidney, Iowa

5.   Assistant to Boys' Dean

6.   President of Association Youth (Hephzibah Faith
      Missionary Association)

7.   Special Outreach Services

8.   Arranging Street Meeting Teams for Tabor,
      Sidney, Malvern, Glenwood

I thanked them and marked the ones I wished to keep. One of the teachers remarked, "We thought you would choose the other four which would give you more time for the school." I ended up keeping all eight.

Before I got my car, I did a lot of hitch-hiking. I had a number of interesting rides. On one occasion I was standing near the highway with my thumb up when a driver pulled up. He almost ran over me when he slammed to a stop. I hurried to get in with him. He really pushed the pedal down. We were up to 50 in a hurry. I kept watching the speedometer. He hit 60, then 70, then 80. When it was nearly up to 90, he said to me, "Say, son, do you want a drink?" He pulled a bottle of liquor out of his pocket. It was nearly empty. I said quickly, "I don't drink!" He tipped the bottle to his lips and at 90 miles an hour emptied it. I was never so frightened in my life. We were approaching a town when he asked, "How far are you going?" I said, "I want off at this next town." It made him mad and he slammed on the brakes. He was off the pavement when he got stopped. When he took off again, his tires threw sand and gravel all over me. I stacked my suitcases and knelt and thanked God I was still in the land of the living.

Volumes could be written of my years at Tabor Bible School. R.L. Gowan was Boys' Dean. We have had many years of friendship since then and many of these were in connection with Indian Missions. Professor George Robbins and his wife Ebba were like my own kin. His mother had taken Mary Alice into their home when she was a girl. (I write about this in Chapter VII) George and Ebba had a daughter and a son born into their home while at Tabor. We went out to see the Christmas lights when Dorothy was a tiny little miss. She couldn't say, "William," but she kept saying, "Pretty 'ights, Wee," which grew into "Uncle Wee." Her brother Paul learned from Dorothy. I am mighty proud of my niece and nephew. We are a close, loving "Uncle Wee" and Aunt Alice. Tabor Bible School with George Robbins as principal furnished me with many fond memories.

Dr. R.E. Carroll taught the subjects "Life of Christ," "First Year Greek," and "Second Year Greek New Testament." I had a car and he didn't. We made many trips together and became brothers in Christ with bonds that equal blood kinship.

Miss Winnie Crouch was my instructor in "Theology." She had an insight into the Word and holy living like very few people I have known. She lived and taught a life of faith that affected my life more than I have words to tell. She was a saint of saints. All four of our children were dedicated by Miss Crouch. I saw the light on Bible standards in her classes. It was both an honor and privilege to join Kathryn Dunn in editing the volume *"Miss Winnie Crouch, A Heroine of Faith."* The Faith Bible College in Mitchell, South Dakota, and the Gospel Center in Phoenix, Arizona, are products of this great saint. Though she never married, she was a true "Mother in Israel."

Mrs. Nellie Williams is another teacher who greatly affected my life. Before writing of her life, I need to tell that I was dismissed seven times from the school. Sister Williams always pled my cause and gained another chance for me. A few years later I was asked to come as president of the school, which I consider a "marvel of marvels"!

I wanted to be certain that returning as president was God's will for me. I said I would return under three conditions: 1) I would need to be treasurer of the school finance. 2) I made a list of a revision of school rules including those pertaining to sensible courtship. 3) Due to my wife's heart weakness, we would need an apartment on first floor.

All I requested was accepted but for one controlling vote. One man was treasurer of the Association and also Missions, Church and School. There were no courtship rules and the apartment they wanted us to move into was upstairs. Since these were my fleeces, I could not accept the position. It was still an honor to be considered.

Mrs. Nellie Williams had lived in Council Bluffs, Iowa. Her husband was on the City Council. They were a society family. Mrs. Williams knew proper etiquette and conduct. Mr. Williams died from a heart attack. She was a broken-hearted lady. As a result, she returned from the funeral to lock her doors, pull the shades and refused to answer either the doorbell or phone. After days of weeping, she realized she was being unfair to her little daughter, Alice J.

Her testimony was that she fell over on the bed and wept and prayed, "Dear God in heaven, could you heal a broken-hearted woman?" Instantly, she felt healing go through her body. Then her prayer was, "Lord, you healed me, now what do you want me to do?" Suddenly, she sensed the Lord was directing her to go to the Bible School at Tabor, Iowa and teach. She packed suitcases for herself and little daughter. Fixing herself up as best as she knew how with a frilly dress and carefully applied cosmetics, she was ready to start her journey to Tabor with her little girl.

She had not known of the Bible School, but felt sure of the leading of the Lord. She and Alice J. took a short bus trip to Tabor. She inquired and found there was a Bible School and I think taxied out the short mile to the school. Elder Weaver, the president, was in for a shock. The school had a strict dress code. It would have been interesting to see his reaction to Nellie Williams' announcement that the Lord had sent her to the school to teach.

Elder Weaver told her he did not know how to respond if it were the Lord who had sent her. He said, "First of all, we do not know you and you are not dressed like any of our ladies. They do not wear junk like you have." Mrs. Williams asked, "What do you mean junk?" She pointed to her necklace and said, "Do you mean these? They are real pearl. My rings are diamonds and gold. If these are not worn here, I can take them off." She did that and put them in her purse. Elder Weaver said, "But you are all painted up." She took her handkerchief and started wiping her face and lips and said, "It will take some water to get rid of all of this." He complained about her frilly dress. "I'll have to have some new dresses made then," she replied.

The president did not know what to say since Nellie Williams responded so quickly. She insisted that God had sent her. Elder Weaver decided God must be in it and accepted her as a teacher. They soon learned that this society lady was a remarkable person.

In the classroom, Sister Williams endeared herself to us and proved to be an exemplary Christian and a wonderful teacher. Because I was a bewildered young person, she manifested a special love and care for me.

60

She helped me overcome my slang and improper language. I said many times, "That teacher loves me." Her very presence influenced the staff.

Several times and for various reasons, I was called before the faculty and dismissed from school. Each time I thanked them for their kindness and headed to my room to pack. During my first two years at school, it had been the same. Dismissed and pack up!

Then Sister Williams would go to prayer. She would call the staff back together and again and again tell them, "There is some good in that boy! We've got to give him another chance." They would then ask me if I could do differently. I would put my shoulders back and with a salute say, "Scouts honor!" I really meant not to pull another prank.

Orville Tweedy brought 3 big fire crackers to the school. We lit one and put it under a can. It sounded like a bomb and blew the can nearly out of sight. One of those nights a fire cracker went off in the girls' dormitory. We went to bed in a hurry and pretended we were asleep. When a search team came and shined a light in our room, I heard one of them say that it wasn't us as we were asleep.

Some weeks later I came into the office to do some printing and heard a serious discussion taking place. I stood in the hall to listen. Someone said, "It's a sure thing it has to be Daniel, Orville and William." Someone else said, "We had better send one of them home to make an example out of them." I thought maybe I was going to win. Another spoke up and said, "It will be too difficult to pick the one most guilty. If we send one, we ought to send them all." I knew that somehow it had leaked out as to who had thrown the fire cracker into the girls' dorm. I hurried up to our dorm to inform Daniel and Orville that we would all have to go home.

I said to Orville, "I think I know a good place to shoot off your last fire cracker. Right where I was just standing! We could shoot it off and then hurry to our rooms and pack for the trip." Orville and Daniel thought that would be a good idea so Orville went to his room to get it. When he came back, Dr. Norman Bonner (we called him Neal then) came out of his room and said, "Boys, I just heard your plot. I want that fire cracker!" Orville said he had good money in it, but he must have sold it to Bro. Bonner. It turned out that none of us were sent home after all. Nellie Williams had prayed and interceded for us. We three boys were grounded for some time and also had to work some extra hours without pay.

After this episode, Neal Bonner and his wife Gertrude went to Africa as missionaries. The Wesleyan Church brought them home to serve as president of Bartlesville College in Oklahoma after they had served a number of terms. I was at the college as evangelist for a revival meeting and Dr. Bonner introduced me by telling of the best investment he had ever made in the purchase of a fire cracker for 10 cents.

At lunch time, on a Monday noon not long after the fire cracker event, one of the teachers remarked, "Sister Williams did not come to her classes this morning. I wonder if something is wrong?" The school president's wife, Mrs. J.M. Zook, slipped out and went to Nellie Williams' upstairs apartment next to the dining room. She came back screaming, "Sister Williams is dead!" It was such a shock that every one fell to their knees in prayer. I said everyone, but there was one boy who felt so unworthy that he ran to the barn without stopping. He climbed up under some hay in the haymow. There he lay and wept for hours. You know who it was without my confessing. I met God there. I reminded the Lord that Nellie Williams loved me. I would try to make up to her and to the Lord by living a dedicated life for others. I have sought from that day to this to be true to that vow. Many times in foreign lands and even in our land, I have asked the Lord to credit Sister Nellie Williams for people making heaven as a result of my preaching.

In our classes Sister Williams often told of her coming to Tabor and how on occasions she would take a weekend to fast and pray for the students and staff of the school and also for the pastors and missionaries. Friday evening, all day Saturday and all day Sunday she would spend in this manner. It was a time of sweet devotion. She would say, "It will be on a Monday morning when I start to get up that the Lord will speak to me and say, 'Nellie, we've had a wonderful weekend. I want you to come up to heaven with me.'" She would go on to say to us, "When you come to see about me, my feet will be over the side of the bed. I'll still be in my night clothes, but I'll not be there. I'll be with my Lord."

Do you remember I have written that it was on a Monday morning? Several of the staff did go over to see Sister Williams. She had a sweet smile on her face, her feet were over the side of the bed as if she were ready to get up. She was right. She was with her Lord!

I am certain heaven has a special place for Nellie Williams. It is one of the first places I wish to go when I get to the city. She loved me. Rev. J.M. Zook preached her funeral. When she was taken to the cemetery for burial, I heard the funeral director say to Rev. Zook, "You have suffered a great loss!" His reply was something like this, "Heaven alone knows how much."

Just think! If it had not been for Rev. Rambo's letter, the Sunday School Superintendent's coming to our boxcar home and hauling us to Sunday School and Miss Lenore Ball putting her arm around me to keep me in Sunday School, this page could not have been written.

I wish, also, to mention Mrs. Staples, who provided a train ride to Tabor. The second year I attended Bible School she informed me that they had a good car. She didn't know how to drive, but could shift gears. I said I could drive, but didn't know how to shift gears. We decided to pool our abilities. I would drive and she would shift gears. We even drove through Omaha, Nebraska. I drove and she shifted gears. By the time we arrived, we both could drive and shift gears. We got so good that we even started waving at bystanders. Anyhow, we arrived at Tabor Bible School where Sister Nellie Williams pled my cause six times, seven times because it must be a perfect number!

7

Life Commitments

William and Alice Kathryn on their Wedding Day

I have made the statement that I have had two girl friends and married them both. I was referring to Mary Alice Ward and Alice Kathryn Jones. I want to tell you about them.

Arriving at Tabor Bible School, I believed I saw the most beautiful girls in all the world. Long hair is beautiful and modest dress graces the figure. Christian training adorns the character. My heart said, "I want one of these for my wife." I was becoming acquainted with beautiful womanhood. Painted dolls were cheap, artificial looking persons to me.

When I met Mary Alice Amelia Ward, at one glance I felt she was the girl for me. She had beautiful black hair. She was slender, but not skinny. She had a lady-like dignity that I liked. But at the Bible School, the fellows were allowed only to give proper greetings or speak of important matters to the girls. Quick salutes and smiles were almost a violation. Mary Alice and I said a lot through our smiles.

Near the close of our high school senior year, I broke the rule by writing her a note. It said, "Mary Alice, I would like to correspond with you this summer when we'll not be breaking the rules. I don't want you to break the rules by writing an answer. Just nod your head when you see me and that will be enough." I had John Rosentrater deliver the note. Later I teased her by saying she hadn't needed to bow double. She did give a lady-like nod that went through me from the tip of my head to the soles of my feet.

When Brother Rosentrater got home from a trip, he gave John a pad and pencil and had him write down all the rules he had broken while his father was away. He wrote, "I gave Mary Alice a note from William." As a result, Mary Alice was instructed to study and do her school assignments in her dormitory room for 3 days. My offense was worse than hers, so I had to study in my room for a week. However, it turned out to be in our favor, since I could see the girls' dorm from my window and she could see the boys' dorm from her desk. We sat with our desks facing the window and an occasional wave back and forth helped us to study better.

The next school year, I said to Sister Williams, "The love bug bit me and I've got a tickling around my heart I can't scratch." She said, "Tut! Tut! Son, that is against the school rules." "I don't want to break the school rules, but I want to have some permission for contact with Mary Alice," I replied. For the school year, we were permitted to write once every six weeks and make our exchange through the girls' matron. Our notes were about the size of a Montgomery Ward catalog. I even read between the lines!

I got it arranged so we could meet for a date at George Robbins' house. It was after school hours. At the time of our first date, I didn't have much of a crop of whiskers, but I shaved and put on perfume before

I milked the cows in the morning. I came home, shaved and perfumed again at noon and then again before my date. I was told not to let the students know about the date. In plenty of time, I walked ½ mile to the west and one mile to the south, ½ mile to the east and ½ mile to the north. I came across the school pasture and arrived at Robbins' at 3:45 P.M. Mr. Robbins said, "William, you're 15 minutes early, what will we do?" I replied, "You better let me in or someone will see me and squeal." I got some extra time. I had bought a box of candy for Mary Alice. I helped her open it so we could enjoy some of it together. We managed to have two more dates before Christmas. We got special permission to marry at Christmas time. Rev. J.M. Zook, Miss Winnie Crouch and Mr. George Robbins gave the approval. We used the Christmas decorations for our wedding. My brother Kenneth owed me $50.00. With that amount I bought our furniture and paid for our wedding and honeymoon.

We sent out our wedding announcements about the first of December. Pearl Harbor was December 7, 1941. Our wedding was set for December 19. I went to Rev. Zook to see if he thought it would be wise to change the date. He felt we should go through with it as planned. We had all prayed about it. We went to my home town in North Platte, Nebraska for our honeymoon. My sister and her husband, Glen and Florence (Pat) Jergensen, went to stay with other relatives and let us use their new home. We appreciated this gesture. My family rather wined and dined us. The time went quickly and soon we were back at the school. A nice one-room apartment was made available to us. I had bought all of our furniture at bargain prices: a small cook stove with white oven door and white warming oven (used also to heat our apartment); a little white cupboard for dishes; and some nice orange and apple boxes for dressers. I bought a bedstead with springs and mattress. So that our furniture would match, I painted the bedstead white. Some of the ladies made curtains for the front of our wooden box dressers. I got carpets for the floor and really worked to make our apartment nice.

Now we were back from our honeymoon and I gallantly carried my new bride across the threshold. She looked around and began to cry. I have never been able to understand women's whims. I began to cry, too. Then I said, "I am sorry, but I did the best I could. I wanted it to be nice for you." "I'm not crying because I'm sad, I'm crying because I'm happy," Mary Alice made me to understand. "This is my own home, my first home!" Crying and laughing, she threw her arms around me and said, "What's mine is mine and what's yours is mine. It's all mine!" We pranced around together. This was the first time I lifted her to my shoulders.

Mary Alice had been an orphan girl. Arrangements had been made for her and her brother to stay in the home of their great aunt and uncle. One day as she and her brother were quarreling, she overheard her aunt complain about them. Her uncle said, "It won't be long until we get rid of these brats in the spring." Mary Alice ran out of the house weeping without taking anything with her. Out of town she ran and into a deep creek valley and up a treed ravine. She crawled under some brush and wept herself to sleep. When she awoke, she heard someone calling her name. She thought the man that found her had a blood hound. The dog was on a leash and seemed friendly. She told the officials she would not go back to her great aunt and uncle. Mrs. George Robbins, Sr. (Stella) had taken Mary Alice's sister Kathleen as a foster child and was willing to do the same for her. The Robbinses were kind to her and since George Robbins, Jr. was a teacher at Tabor Bible School, she enrolled as a student there.

George Robbins reported to me that when Mary Alice graduated from eighth grade at the Bushnell, South Dakota School, no student had ever topped her grade average.

Mary Alice was a tender, caring person who loved her family and friends and always cherished what the Lord allowed us to possess. She did not have a selfish bone in her body.

Our first pastorate was at Niobrara, Nebraska. The old mission building was an interesting place. The sanctuary faced onto Main Street. At one time it had been a grocery store; then a dance hall; later a bowling alley. The maple lumber was taken apart and used for flooring and the bolt holes were filled with small corks when the building became a saloon. Finally, it became a church and parsonage. Quite a history and quite a conversion! The pulpit I used had been a roulette stand for gambling. The bar was made of beautiful walnut. Openings were cut in it to make doorways for two bedrooms. The counter tops were left in the bedrooms. This worked perfectly for us. Our orange boxes fit under the counter tops and with curtains hung over them, they made storage-like dressers.

The building was old and had no insulation. The ceilings were 12 feet high so it took a lot of fuel to heat. By looking at the curtains, you could tell which way the wind was blowing.

One chilly morning my wife was rather lazy about getting out of bed. Both clad in our cotton pajamas, we scuffled a bit. I finally set her up on the black walnut bar. Then I turned around and pulled her onto my shoulders. Since it was just the two of us, I raced around the long living room giving her a piggy back ride. On one trip around, I pushed the organ stool out into the room. I intended when coming around, to see if I could jump the stool. When Mary Alice realized what I was planning, she went to kicking and got me off balance. I straddled the stool and stumbled along clear over in front of our kitchen door.

The door had a large glass section in it and we had forgotten to pull the blind. There stood the Presbyterian preacher. My wife lit off my shoulders and ended up under the bed covers. I told the preacher we were frolicking a little. He said he believed we were. We had a good laugh. Mary Alice was very agile and could do cart wheels; also both back and forward flips landing on her feet. We learned to pull our blinds!

In *Happy Happenings* I wrote of my wife's healing from a stroke. It was such a miracle that I would like for you to read it. She said of that experience, "William, it was a real awakening to me. Others may get careless, but I don't dare because of my heart condition and the uncertainty of my life. I must be ready to die at any moment."

We were on a tour for the Indian Work when her time came. After suffering a heart attack, she regained consciousness and prayed with me in her concern for the children. She praised the Lord and it was only a short time until she was with her Lord. She was my boyhood sweetheart. I felt the sun had set and would never rise again after we laid her to rest in the Evergreen Cemetery at Hot Springs, South Dakota. I would go there alone to pray. The children wanted a full-sized granite marker with "Mother" engraved on it; then her name. Many a night I lay in bed at home and wept.

In my desperation one night, I drove about 15 miles to the grave site. I stretched out on the cold grave stone. It seemed as if a voice spoke to me, "She is not here, for she is risen." It seemed that the same angel that spoke the words concerning Jesus' resurrection was speaking to me. I felt the cold stone and looking heavenward said aloud, "Thank you, Lord, this grave is empty; she is with you." She would never be an orphan again. There that night I partook of the sorrow that Jesus' mother and His disciples did. I learned anew the meaning of the resurrection. The comfort I gained was something of eternal strength and grace. Now I could endeavor to comfort my own children: "For she is not here: for she is risen."

This chapter is titled "Life Commitments." Marriage is "until death do us part." There are many little souls, but I was married to a big soul. Mary Alice felt this heart attack would be our parting time. She sat in my lap and we had our arms around each other. We were so close that I felt we were breathing together. She talked with me about each of the children. Her final words about all four of them were, "Do your best to get them to heaven. That is my chief burden." She then said, "William, you have given me all of your love. My counsel would be not to wait too long before you marry again."

There were a few times that I prayed, "Why don't you take me to heaven, too, Lord?" Then I would feel the reproof. The children needed their father more than ever. While I was single, it seemed like a ten-year period. Time moved slowly.

Alice Kathryn and I had our courtship and a happy, loving marriage. I learned what an honor and privilege it is to belong to the Frank Jones family. They all welcomed me and the children. Alice has been a wonderful wife and a great mother for my children. Mothers' Day has become a special time for our children to share their love for their step-mother.

Before coming to Brainerd Indian School to teach, Alice had experience teaching in rural one-room schools in Kansas and North Dakota as well as a Christian Day School at Custer, South Dakota. She taught four years at Brainerd. One of those years she was chosen "Teacher of the Year" and featured in the South Dakota Teachers' Journal. Her students had showed the most scholastic improvement of any in the state.

Alice keeps our home neat and plans delicious, inexpensive meals. At one time I had three secretaries; now I have one. If I don't take time to count out the rhythm in my poetry, she comes to my rescue. She proof-reads and corrects my other writing. We have devoted our life commitment to each other.

Around our family altar, she has brought us to our senses at different times by asking forgiveness for her failures. Her devotion is to her Lord and to her family. The Lord says we'll be like angels in heaven. She'll be able to fit in when she arrives in the City.

Life's three most important choices can be listed thus: I. Choice of Christ; II. Choice of Companion; III. Choice of Career. I have written of the first two. Now I write of my career. During my Bible School days, I became concerned about my choice of life's work. I was seeking the Lord during a revival while Rev. Walter Drown was evangelist. I felt the Lord speak to me from Isaiah chapter 12, the shortest chapter in the book. Verses 2 and 3 give my testimony. Verse 2 closes by stating, "The Lord Jehovah is my STRENGTH, MY SONG and my SALVATION." Verse 3 reads, "With joy shall ye draw water out of the wells of salvation." I enjoyed being a Christian. Verse 4 was my call to a career: "And in that day shall ye say,

I.   "Praise the Lord." I sought to do this frequently. This was my call to praise the Lord for what He had done for me personally.

II.   "Call upon His name." Prayer was the medium to grace and spiritual victory. Communion in prayer was the avenue that took me into the presence of God. I found it the means of experiencing His divine miracles. This can be done morning, noon and night. Sometimes I communed with Him all night.

III.   "Declare his doings among the people." How could I do that better than by preaching? We have the GREATEST METHOD – "Declare it"; the GREATEST MESSAGE – "His doings" and the GREATEST MULTITUDE – "The people." This has been my career for well over sixty years.

I was hitch-hiking back to School when a young insurance salesman picked me up and gave me a lengthy ride. He told me about his policy. Then he said, "Maybe you already have insurance." I said, "I do. I have my policy with me." He was surprised that I could carry it in my pocket. "Would you mind showing it to me?" he asked. I said, "It is not so long but what I can read it to you." I had a small new testament with Psalms so I read Psalm 91 to him. (Many scholars believe that Moses wrote both Psalm 90 and 91). I pointed out that my cost was prayer and that it was a Biblical Life Insurance. I mentioned that the angels and God Himself were involved in it. I told him that the best part of it was: "With long life will I satisfy him and show him my salvation." I asked him what he thought of it and he said, "Young man, keep it. Mine doesn't make those kind of promises." He had tears in his eyes when he said it. Now, 64 years later at this writing, it still is viable.

The 91st Psalm has been called the Psalm of Protection as the following incident makes clear: "F.L. Rawson, noted engineer, and one of England's greatest scientists, in his book *LIFE UNDERSTOOD* gives an account of a British regiment under the command of Col. Whitelesey, who served in the World War for more than four years without losing a man. This unparalleled record was made possible by means of active cooperation of officers and men in memorizing and repeating regularly the words of the 91st Psalm."

In 1962 when Alice and I had been married less than a year, we left for a trip to Marion, Indiana for a missionary convention. Just east of Rapid City, South Dakota we came into a blinding snow storm. Our car slid into the ditch and we were stranded. Many cars stopped to give us aid, but we sent them on as we were not cold and it would soon be daylight. It would have been dangerous with the combination of semi-darkness, blizzard and slippery road. However, one driver stopped and we couldn't persuade him to go on. He had parked on the wrong side of the road and insisted that we transfer our luggage into his car and go with him. While we were in the process, another car approached, coming from the same direction we had been traveling. The road was slippery and the driver was unable to keep from slamming into the vehicle into which we were transferring our bags. I saw the oncoming headlights and pushed the trunk lid down, but was hurled onto the pavement and was found several yards down the highway. I was hurt badly, suffering severe head injuries and a concussion. On the way to the hospital, I regained consciousness. A long account could be given. I was hospitalized 18 days.

In my struggle to recover, I thought of my wife. She would be a bride and a widow all in one year if the Lord did not heal me. I prayed and asked the Lord for a promise from the Word. I believe He reminded me that He had given me a full insurance policy. I could quote the 91st Psalm. I remembered: "angels," "long life," "satisfy thee." I was able to trust the Lord. Let me make clear that there was a multitude of family and friends praying for me. I dressed and was released the 18th day.

When we got back to Hot Springs, I went in to see the mayor who was also my insurance agent. He threw up his hands and said, "It was reported to me, Rev. Gale, that you could never recover; I was to write up your policy coverage." I was so happy I could tell him the Lord had changed all of that and healed me. Since that experience, I especially love the comforting song UNDER HIS WINGS.

UNDER HIS WINGS

Under His wings I am safely abiding
Though the night deepens and tempests are wild,
Still I can trust Him: I know He will keep me.
He has redeemed me, and I am His child.

Under His wings what a refuge in sorrow!
How the heart yearningly turns to His rest!
Often when earth has no balm for my healing,
There I find comfort and there I am blest.

Under His wings, O what precious enjoyment!
There will I hide till life's trials are o'er
Sheltered, protected, no evil can harm me.
Resting in Jesus, I'm safe ever-more

Under His wings, under his wings,
Who from His love can sever?
Under His wings my soul shall abide,
Safely abide forever.

Words: William O. Cushing

Music: Ira D. Sankey

He shall cover thee with His feathers, and under His wings shalt thou trust: his truth shall be thy shield and buckler Psalm 91:4.

8

Blessed in Giving and Receiving

M any stories have been told about the depression years. Because of our low financial income during our years of labor among the American Indian, we didn't know when the Depression ended. A car dealer at Rapid City, South Dakota bought a big shipment of automobiles at a very low price. He told me he had lowered his present stock in order to get some cash to keep his business afloat. I wanted a four-door Plymouth. He had what I was looking for and offered me a good deal: low price with no trade-in required. I bought my first car. My, was I happy! I learned later that it was a good thing I hadn't bought one of the large lot of cars he had purchased. They had been stolen and had fake titles. This dealer lost all he had and many customers lost their cars.

I dedicated my new car to the Lord. I took some of the students at Brainerd Indian School with me so we could have prayer together. I told the Lord it was His car. I titled it in the name of the Indian School. As president, I could guard its usage. I endeavored to give it the best kind of care. I purchased a station wagon for our personal use.

A year later, Reverend Neal Phipps and I bought a piece of land and divided it so we each would have a good lot on which to build a house. Actually, we purchased a barracks building which had formerly housed army officers. It had oak floors and good siding. When painted, one would not have guessed its original usage. We divided the building in the middle. We each partitioned our part into kitchen-dining area, living room, 3 bedrooms and 2 baths. On one end of ours we built an apartment for my mother. We never lived in the house, but felt the Lord wanted us to sell it and put the money into Indian Missions. We have been asked if we hadn't had a struggle giving both our car and house to the Lord. Our main struggle was to be certain we had done what the Lord wanted us to do. We have found that one doesn't get ahead of the Lord. He has made it up to us in many, many ways.

Since I have mentioned cars, I would like to tell more about them. While pastoring in Rawlins, Wyoming, the City Council voted me "preacher of the year." The funds had been raised and a new Ford car was to be given to me. I received a call from the Ford Garage to come and get my car; it was ready. I told them I was moving and didn't feel it would be fair to take it and move away. I had already accepted the position of president of Brainerd Indian School.

They insisted that I come and look at it. If I felt I couldn't take it, I would need to sign the title as it was made out in my name. They wanted me to drive it, and I said I was afraid I might be tempted to get out of the will of the Lord. The car was a shiny, black Ford; a beauty with air conditioning and all the bells and whistles of that day. This was my second new car and I was returning it. I certainly felt honored in what the city had felt to do for me. The camera crew was there. I did wonder if I should take it, but resisted the temptation.

When we returned to the Indian School as president, we were so busy keeping things going that we hardly had time to think of a vehicle for travel. Whatever automobiles the school had, we were free to use. We tried to keep them in repair and ready to go. Mr. Bob Harris, from the Harris Ford Center in Hot Springs, called and said, "Rev. Gale, I want you to get your friend Neal Phipps and come in. I want to talk cars with you." I got Neal Phipps and we went to see Bob Harris. Both Reverend Phipps and I were spending much of our time clutching steering wheels, pushing gas pedals and heading down the highways.

Bob Harris said, "I want you men to give me your old cars. Will you do it?" We knew him well enough to trust him. Both of us nodded our heads and said, "Yes." He said, "I want you men to drive Fords. I'll put you in new Fords and sell yours for you. I don't want you to put more than 50,000 miles on the cars before you turn them in. Understand this, there is no other dealer involved in this. We'll not make a cent. There are lots of people who work with the American Indian, but you men are effective in what you do. I want to help you do it. Is this a fair deal?" We exclaimed, "We know it is more than fair." For many years we both got our cars from Harris Ford Center. Each of us chalked up such high mileage that one year we would drive one car and the next year two cars. We figured we spent $600.00 a year. That was a very excellent dividend for the two cars I had given for the Lord's work. There is a big "Hallelujah, Praise the Lord" in my soul. God takes care of His own.

I pastored two churches for a while: one at Tuthill, South Dakota and the other in the Sandhills at Eli, Nebraska. Along with that, I taught a small town school at Patricia, South Dakota. It was my responsibility to teach all eight grades, so some of the classes had to be combined in order to work them into the time schedule. There were two ex-teachers who had children in the school.

The Dakota Conference of the Wesleyan Methodist Church invited us to pioneer a church at Hot Springs, South Dakota. We prayed about it and felt we should, so we made the move. After we had been gone two years, the Patricia School Board sent two of its members to Hot Springs to ask us to return. They had divided the school into two rooms with two teachers and were prepared to change back to one room with one teacher. They would give me both checks. In addition, they wanted us to pastor a community church that would bring a separate salary. One of the men said that he personally would give us ten, or as many acres as we wanted, for a house and yard. As a community, the ranchers would go together and build the house and pay for it. Anything they couldn't do themselves, they would hire done. With this accomplished, they would bring their trucks and move us. These families could and would have done it if we had agreed. It was not that we were so great, but they loved us. But there was One that we loved more dearly and He wanted us to pioneer a church in Hot Springs. We could not be in two places at once.

Giving and Receiving is the title of this chapter. Many times I have told of the little town of Tuthill, South Dakota and of our moving there to pastor. Mr. Tuthill was still living at that time. He was a kind, elderly man who owned a grocery store. A counter stretched across the front of the store. There was a Dutch door at one end. The top half was always open. The bottom half had to be opened to get to where the groceries were. This was a common arrangement for stores in those days. You would come to the counter and the clerk would go and get what you wished to buy. When Mr. Tuthill died, the Wilbur Case family purchased the store. When they needed to be away, I often clerked for them. By means of the store and the church, I became well acquainted in the community. It was my privilege to make calls in all of their homes.

Mr. C.O. Dennison was a wealthy rancher. He was a member of the Presbyterian Church, but came faithfully to our Sunday evening services. One day he came by and said, "Reverend Gale, if you would have time, I want to take you for a ride." I said I would, so we drove to the rim of the Sandhills. In fact we turned around so we could see the valley and land area through which we had just come. When not in church, I called him "C.O." and he called me "William." He said, "William, do you see that large grass valley and those ranch buildings?" It was as nice a ranch setup as you could find anywhere. He continued, "That grass land is sub-irrigated and furnishes enough hay for several head of cattle with enough left over to sell. In dry years as well as in wet years, it is all the same, all the prairie hay one would need. Now, do you see the farm land? It always raises big crops of corn. Never fear, it would corn-feed the cattle. One more thing, those hills are such that cattle can graze and still find shelter from storms no matter from which direction they come."

He was right! Beautiful farm buildings; an ideal large ranch. He said that it was all his and paid for, but he had sold it and had the money. He went on to say, "My daughter and her husband Russell are well-fixed. They do not need money. Now, this is my concern. What should I do with my money? This is a far greater problem than when I had it tied up in the ranch and cattle. I have been lying awake nights thinking and even praying about it. This is where you come into the picture. I would like to build and invest the money so that it will be a blessing to this community."

He continued, "I hear you preach and I like it. I see you handle the Tuthill store. You know how to meet people. I feel you can handle money. Now, this is what I want to do. I want to build a big store to handle all kinds of products: groceries, hardware, farm equipment, drugs and medical supplies. This will be far more than a million dollar operation. I'll fully stock this store." He had described a Kmart or Walmart type store long before they came into existence.

Mr. Dennison stated, "This will be yours on only one condition: you will stay here to supervise it. Should it fail, that's my risk and you dissolve it as seems best to you. The reason I ask you to consider this program is that I want you to understand it and then pray about it before you give me an answer."

I thought to myself, "I couldn't even consider such a program, let alone own and be in charge of it." On our way back to Tuthill, he assured me, "William, I will still love you whatever you decide." When I prayed, I said, "Lord, I know you called me to preach and I couldn't do it with all that money and a big store hanging around my neck. I'll kindly tell him 'No,' if you'll bless me!" God did, and I felt oceans of love for C.O.

Dennison, but nothing to turn me away from telling the gospel story. When I prayed, the Lord witnessed to my heart. I knew that earthly riches were not the love of my life.

I told C.O., "If the Lord called me to some other place, I would not want anything to hinder His marching orders." His reply to me was, "I knew that would be your answer. I am happy that you have that kind of devotion." And we did remain good friends!

When we pastored in Rawlins, Wyoming, it was a real challenge. The city grew rapidly due to an oil boom. The church was in a favorable location. The people in that section of the town were poor, but some of the church members had jobs with good incomes. Most of them drove in from a distance. My predecessor was a good pastor and successful in visitation. When some of them got saved, he would take them into full membership before they were really ready. They needed more discipling. Attendance records were made that were hard to beat. I kept a written account of my calls. As best as I could calculate, I called at every home in the city. My Uncle John purchased a ranch just west of Rawlins. I loved my time with these relatives. Through Uncle John I got acquainted with the mayor of the city. Quite often I would go to his office and chat with him. The last year we pastored in Rawlins, we had a good growth.

Dr. Swauger, chairman of the Church Extension Department of the Wesleyan Methodist Church, talked with me and said he felt I must come back to the Indian Work. I really wanted to give at least one more year to the pastorate in Wyoming. Dr. Swauger felt if I didn't come, he would have to recommend the closing of the Brainerd Indian School. After special prayer, I consented to return.

My resignation was met with strong objections and an effort to get us to stay. One of our church members worked as a maid for Mrs. Isadore Bolton, a wealthy Jewish lady. The Boltons had moved into the area when cattle men and sheep men were having problems over grazing areas. Sheep eat the grass shorter than cattle so they can't be pastured together. The Boltons bought up lots of land. The ranch through which the Platte River flowed was the smallest of their three ranches. It was about 15 miles square. They referred to it as their little ranch. They also owned the big shearing sheds and pens at Dad, Colorado. Also, if they didn't own it, they held the controlling shares of one of the high-rise skyscrapers along Lake Michigan in Chicago. Mr. Bolton had passed away before we moved to Wyoming.

We often made pastoral calls on Mrs. Bolton's maid, Evelyn Pidcock. Most often it turned into a visit with Mrs. Bolton. When we were considering moving back to Brainerd, she joined with our church group in trying to keep us in Rawlins. She thought our problem was financial and she would contact our church board to see what they could pay for salary. She would add to the amount so as to make a good increase. Also, she would start out by putting $5,000.00 in our checking account.

Since I had talked with her so much about Israel and since she had relatives there, she would take my wife and me on a much better tour than any commercial travel group. We still declined and returned to the Indian School with no promised salary. Years later my wife and I visited Mrs. Bolton at the high-rise building in Chicago.

Over the years, God has taken care of us and I feel we have been much happier in depending on the Lord for our support. We have a great debt to the Houghton College Church in New York and the Shelbyville Bible Holiness Church in Indiana for their support. The Evangelistic Tabernacle in Cooperstown, Pennsylvania has cared for our Brotherhood and Samaritan Ministries Health Share programs for the past several years.

We pastored some very dear people in northern Michigan just before moving to Edinburgh, Indiana. The Tom Clark family: Tom, Edith and Joanna set aside $10,000.00 from their sawmill assets to cushion our missionary work while we were missionary secretary for the Bible Methodist Church. During the sixteen years we served in that capacity, we drew on this fund many times. This helped my wife and me to sleep better knowing there were funds for emergency needs of the fields. We do not have words to express how much this meant to us. Knowing that God had impressed them as a family to help us in this way was such a lift. We could pray over needs whether small or great and God would still take care of them. He was hearing us when we prayed and we witnessed many very special answers. God enabled us to raise the funds to pay back the loans.

These accounts of "Giving and Receiving" have been remarkable highlights in our lives. Some even reveal tests that we needed. These kept us trusting the Lord. He was the one who asked us to "Go ye into all the world and preach the gospel to every creature and, lo, I am with you always even unto the end of the age."

9

Acceptance with the Dakotas

Mrs. Frances Montour Is Potawatomi. Rev. Raymond Montour Was a
Delaware. They Founded the Society of Indian Missions with
Headquarters in Winner, South Dakota.

*I*n the previous chapter I told of our call and moving to
Niobrara, Nebraska to pastor. Our first acquaintance was with
a Sioux Indian by the name of Johnny Godfrey. His first words
to us were, "I have been waiting for you to arrive so I could help you
unload your stuff. I am one of the Indians who attends the church." We
worked together until I was interrupted for some reason. When I came
back, he had both the car and trailer unloaded. He had picked up the
heavy stoves and furniture with little effort. I doubt if I have ever met a
stronger man. Just before he went home, he patted me on the shoulder,
slipped something into my pocket and hastened out the door.

When we arrived at Niobrara, we had only 57 cents left. The three dollar bills from Johnny seemed like a lot of money in 1941. A bond of Christian love was born in those first few minutes with this kind Indian friend. The physical boost and love offering were really needed and appreciated.

Since this man and his wife Ivy were so helpful and influential in our acceptance by the Sioux, I would like to relate his testimony: Pastor Ivan Turner, my predecessor to the Niobrara pastorate, related the story of Johnny's conversion to me. He told me that when the police had to arrest him it would take three or four officers to handle him.

When Johnny came to the parsonage on one occasion, he was so intoxicated that he could hardly walk. He requested Rev. Turner to take him home. The pastor said he would be glad to, but his wife was gone with the car. He volunteered to help him walk home. They started walking at the edge of State Highway 12. It was hard for Rev. Turner to keep Johnny from falling. He kept staggering out into the middle of the road.

Rev. Turner was afraid a car would run into them. He stopped Johnny and told him that he should let God save him. His reply was, "Do you think God would save a drunken Indian like me?" The pastor was grateful for John 3:16. He quoted it and told Johnny that this included him. Then Johnny said, "I want to pray and get saved."

Rev. Turner advised Johnny, "When we get to your house we'll pray." He insisted that he wanted to do it right then. He got down on his knees in the middle of the highway and started to pray. Rev. Turner said the cars were passing on both sides of them and that it scared all the prayer out of him. He flagged cars and tried to pray. Johnny continued to seek the Lord until he prayed through. The Lord sobered him up and he told the pastor he felt so good about it that he could now make it on his own. The two walked on to Johnny's home. His wife was beyond herself with joy. As far as I know, Johnny never touched liquor again.

I took my Indian friend with me on different trips to give his testimony. He so humbly honored the Lord as he witnessed to the saving grace of God. People attending the services were moved on and many wept as Johnny tenderly told of his transformation by the wonderful Lord and Savior. Our own church folk loved him and loved to hear his testimony.

He was unique in telling his story. One time he wanted us to know that this salvation was something down inside. As he unbuttoned his coat, he said, "It is something you get inside your coat." Unbuttoning his vest, he said, "It is something you get inside of your vest." He continued, "You get it inside your shirt." He unbuttoned two or three buttons and pointed inside his shirt, saying, "You get it inside your old dirty underwear." He went on to say, "You get it inside your hide; in fact, you get it way down in your heart." This produced a little laughter, but his testimony was so real to him that the spirit of the Lord moved the congregation to weeping and praising God. His salvation was a marvel of the redeeming grace of the Lord.

The thing that helped us most was that the Godfreys knew their Indian people so well that they arranged for us to have weeknight services in their homes. My wife baked many chocolate cakes for refreshments after the home services. Many got saved in their homes and others in our church.

I spoke for the Indian wakes and also preached for many funerals. In the Indian homes, I sometimes had services with the Catholic priests. On one occasion, a priest by the name of Bears Heart and I were together for the dedication of a child. He asked me, "Which do you want to do; speak or have the prayers?" I replied, "You are the older of us two; you make the choice." He said, "I'll speak." He laid his prayer book beside me. I ignored the manual and prayed for the child, the family and especially for the parents. When I was finished, Bears Heart said, "We'll pray again." His prayer was accented a few times with the expression "Through our Lord Jesus Christ, Amen." The family said "Amen" with him.

Bears Heart then delivered a sermon about ten minutes in length. When he was finished, I said, "We'll speak again." I got up and he sat down. My sermon was about the same length as his. When we were alone, I said, "Bears Heart, don't ever treat me like that again. You knew I wouldn't use your prayer book." He smiled and put his arm around my shoulder. He understood me and we remained friends and walked away together.

I have related some happenings that helped us to become accepted by the Indians. There is some history of Indian missions that I wish to relate which turned out to be a major key to our acceptance with the Santee Sioux.

After receiving a 3-year diploma for a Christian Workers' Course, I worked on my studies for the Bachelor of Sacred Literature. This was conferred in 1951. We moved to the pastorate at Niobrara, Nebraska, which was located where the Niobrara River flows into the Missouri. The Santee Sioux Agency was located about 15 miles northeast of Niobrara.

In 1870, the Albert Riggs family came from Illinois to develop a high school and normal training institute at Santee. There was a small house and a few shacks when their labors in building began. By the time we moved into the area, the schools were closed, but the buildings were still good and the campus was beautiful. The Riggs became a loved family after a period of rejection by the Sioux.

Recently it was my privilege to purchase a book titled *MARY and I: FORTY YEARS with the SIOUX (1837-1877)* by Dr. Stephen Riggs. This book revealed the harsh treatment that Stephen and Mary went through in efforts to win the Sioux for Christ. They were instrumental in getting workers to help them start about 50 churches for Indians in Wisconsin, Minnesota, and North and South Dakota.

Nina Foster Riggs came to the area and worked with the women and children. Thomas Riggs was married after he came to the field and he and his wife operated the Hope Mission. Both Santee and Niobrara locations are now covered by back waters from Fort Randal Dam on the Missouri River.

Stephen Riggs tells of riding a grey pony and stopping at Bazille Creek. This was about 6 miles east of Niobrara. This is where Albert and Willie Frazier and nephew David Frazier made eulogies when they took me into the Santee tribe. It was my honor to sit in and take part in their tribal meetings. They all spoke in the Dakota Sioux language and I only know a little of it. I was limited in what I could understand. When I preached, I had to use an interpreter so this limited me, also. When we moved to Niobrara, Albert and Willie were very aged. David was the tribal chairman. Dan and Cornelia Frazier were close neighbors and had a larger house than most Indians. They were very hospitable and made their home available for many funeral wakes. I spoke there for many other special events. Whether in their home or in other homes, the Catholic priests were expected to speak also. In those days, it was the custom that family and friends sit with the dead until after the funeral. This gave us a close relationship with many Indian families in the area.

Back in 1865, Indian prisoners held at Davenport, Iowa were released by order of President Abraham Lincoln. They came to Niobrara where they met their families. Due to spiritual revival in the prison, some of these men were licensed to preach and were the key to a great revival in many areas where the American Indian Church Movement had already built churches.

There are at least two major reasons for the information regarding Stephen and Mary Riggs. First, it gives a real life picture of the price they paid to take the gospel to the Indians. Second, it shows how that love service and sacrifice paid off in a very effective and wide-spread revival.

Two generations later, we came to Niobrara where the revival had begun among the Sioux. A few of the old Indians remembered the Riggs families. Most everyone knew about them, but had forgotten the harsh treatment that was given them. The Indian leaders felt we were much like the Riggs in our special love and care for them. They decided right away to be kind to us. We had lived there about a year when they welcomed me into their tribe. I did not know of this background until later years.

This respect and honor carried over into our leadership at Brainerd Indian School. Much could be written of this esteem given us while others had to work to earn it. We have had the privilege of being on many mission fields where we fell in love with the people, but I think the Indian Work was most dear because it was our first love.

After Albert Riggs could no longer carry on the Santee Normal School, it was closed because of lack of leadership to the churches and there was a falling away in their endurance and in their church attendance.

That was the background when a committee came to see us at Brainerd. They said if we could give leadership to those churches, they would legally give all of them to us. It would have been too much for us to keep up financially along with the leadership of Brainerd Indian School. I have always regretted that we were unable to shoulder this responsibility and help lead these churches for the Indians' sake. This offer came only a couple of years before Raymond Montour came to South Dakota and established the Society of Indian Missions. I believe I could have guided them in that direction. I was so much under the load of the Brainerd Indian School that I failed in a great opportunity for church building for those dear Dakota Indians.

10
Among Many Tribes

INDIAN CULTURE

Some of the tribes place food on the graves of their departed loved ones. One Pale Face asked a Native American, "When will your loved one come back to eat the food?" His reply was, "When yours comes back to see and smell your flowers." Culture is not wrong unless it violates the Word of God.

Indian Salutation

The smoke is gathering o'er my tepee.

The tent flap is hanging open.

Let's look into each other's eyes and shake hands together.

The wah-cod-yah-pe★ is steaming hot; let's drink together.

The sun is shining warm; let's sit together.

We want to be good friends; let's talk together.

The trials and burdens are great; let's share together.

The sorrows and heartaches are many; let's care together.

The burdens are lightened by a smile; let's laugh together.

*The trees are whispering; the brooks are murmuring, and the hills are beckoning;
let's walk together.*

*The journey may be long, our moccasins are worn, the ponies are swift;
let's ride together.*

*Down hill, up hill, over hill, and all through life.
We are friends forever, together.*

★· *Peh-zoo-tah-sah-pah and wah-cod-yah-pe are both Sioux words for coffee.*

– Chief Hugs Himself

There are varying figures as to the number of Indian tribes and Indian lands in the United States. This is because these represent many parcels of land which have been inhabited by Indians in the past, but no longer are. Some include the Eskimos and Aleuts; other census recordings do not. I have read that there are 250 to 325. However many there are, you will find that each tribe has its own particular culture. In one given year at Brainerd Indian School, there were 17 tribes represented in the student body. At that time we had had a total of 34 different tribes since the school's beginning. They had come from many of our states as well as from Canada.

Some of the tribes place food on the graves of their departed loved ones. One Pale Face asked a Native American, "When will your loved one come back to eat the food?" His reply was, "When yours come back to see and smell the flowers." Cultures are not wrong unless they violate the Word of God. Indians of all lands hold their elderly in high esteem. Also they have great respect for their land. They make loyal soldiers and friends.

John Sitting Bull, a grandson of the famed Sitting Bull, came to our campus many times. On one occasion he wanted to borrow money to buy gasoline. He spoke through an interpreter. We had a gas pump for school use. I had started a kind of pawn shop for the Indian people if they didn't have the money and needed to purchase something. They were to leave something of value with me for security. I told John that was the only way I could loan money. But since we were such good friends, I would give him three dollars worth of gas. He got so excited that he said, "Oh thank you so much." It was in perfect English. I laughed and told him he forgot his interpreter. He laughed and said, "I sure did."

A short time before this, the Bureau of Indian Affairs sent John and a couple other elderly Indian men to Washington, D.C. On the return trip, the air pressure went down in the plane and released his hearing. He had been deaf for many years. I got acquainted with John Sitting Bull when I handled the food commodity programs for Custer and Fall River Counties. Our Brainerd staff worked with me.

On one of my trips to Navajo land, my brother Kenneth volunteered to drive for me. He was full of fun and told me that if there were any remarks made about his driving, he would be the one to make them. Along the way, the police stopped him for driving too fast in a school zone. The officer asked to see his driver's license. Kenneth was a husky chap and four years my senior. He was asked regarding the 200 pounds recorded on his license. His answer was, "That's what I weighed when I got my license. I didn't see any need to change that; it's like your name!" The policeman grinned at Kenneth and he got away with only a reproof.

He had not driven much further when he drove too close in front of a patrol car. Again he was stopped with only a reproof. Kenneth complained that the cops were picking on him. When we arrived a bit late, I explained that my brother had lost a lot of time because of traffic violations.

Kenneth thought we had missed our dinner. The Navajos can include a lot of things in their services. This was my brother's first time to be with them. After several special songs were dedicated to "Dear Brother Gale," Kenneth finally thought, "Dear Brother Gale" should be "Deer Buck Gale" and should be shot. Then we could go and eat! At about three o'clock in the afternoon, it was time for dinner. Brother Kenneth felt his little intestines had nearly eaten his big ones. After some good mutton stew, he was in better humor.

When it was time for the next service, Kenneth said, "I'm ready to go hear some more 'Dear Brother Gale' specials." It was always a happy and interesting occasion to be with the Navajos. Their tribe is the largest in our country.

The Pueblo tribes also live in Southwest United States. They are village dwellers. It is a treat to eat bread from their outdoor ovens. Especially when it is hot and spread with butter!

On one occasion when we were with the Seminoles in Florida, we were able to get a beautiful many-colored, two-piece dress for my wife. These dresses are made by sewing tiny pieces of material into colorful patterns. It takes many hours to make a dress. We saw them sit at their tables in their grass-roofed cottages and sew with treadle machines. Chickens, ducks and dogs went in and out at leisure. The dress we purchased is on display in the Gale Mission Center at God's Bible School in Cincinnati, Ohio. It is interesting to read of Osceola, the famous Seminole Chief, and his people from the Everglades of Florida. This tribe has never signed a treaty with the U.S. Government. Theirs is a distinctive way of life.

The Iroquois, an Algonquian Language Group, is a compilation of Oneida, Mohawk, Huron, Tuscarora and Cherokee. This includes a confederation of six nations or tribes: Seneca, Cayuga, Onondaga, Oneida, Mohawk, and Tuscarora. These tribes are found in upstate New York. The well-known Tom Claus Mohawk family are from this area. We are acquainted with at least a few from all of these tribes. We were best known by the Onondagas.

Rev. Raymond Montour was from the Delaware tribe in Ontario, Canada. He served for many years as president of the Society of Indian Missions. This tribe is distinct from the Iroquois, but perhaps are cousins. I was in the Philippines when Rev. Montour passed away. I was not able to make it for his funeral. His wife, Mrs. Frances Montour, is a Potawatomi from Michigan.

Rev. Blanchard Jimerson was a great preacher from the Seneca tribe. He also served as vice president of the Society of Indian Missions. He was in his own home area of Jimersontown, New York when he passed away. It was blizzarding and I couldn't arrange a flight and was fearful of driving so I was unable to speak for his funeral. Mrs. Jimerson is also from the Seneca tribe. Rev. Montour and Rev. Jimerson were equal and beyond most of us Pale Face preachers. They make heaven seem nearer and more precious to me.

I would like to report on some students who attended Brainerd Indian School who have become leaders:

Oliver Hill became a leader for the Onondaga Tribe near Syracuse, New York. Harry Logan, a graduate from our Bible Department, became a chosen chief for an Eastern Seneca Tribe. Calvin (Cabby) Jimerson became mayor of Salamanca, New York. Jim Northrup became a speaker and leader from the Ojibway (Chippewa) tribe in Cloquet, Minnesota. His home is on the Fon Du Lac Indian Reservation. Betty Stewart (Eadie), a Sioux from South Dakota, speaks on radio and television and appears in special news articles relating her death experience and restoration to life. She has written at least two books. Her home is in Woodenville, Washington.

I'll name a few others of our students who have done well: Jerry (Sioux from South Dakota) and Johanna (Onondaga from New York) Yellowhawk live at Black Hawk, South Dakota. They are special to us as I had the honor of speaking the vows at their wedding. Jerry and Becky Wakeman are residing at Winner, South Dakota. He is Sioux from South Dakota and Becky is Delaware-Potawatami. This touches only a few who have been successful.

On our 2003 trip to South Dakota we saw Cecelia Fast Horse (now Spotted Bear) who is from the Sioux Tribe. She is doing a great work in her home community at Wounded Knee, South Dakota. We were also privileged to see David Delgarito who has done a lot of art work for us. He is a Navajo who now lives in South Dakota.

This chapter is titled "Among Many Tribes." On one of our Alabama trips, we were at Atmore with the Martin Gehmans for revival meetings.

This was several moons ago. It was a real highlight to be with them and is a highlight still remembered. Mrs. Gehman is from the Eastern Creek Band. Her parents were one of the sweetest couples we have met. The Gehmans' three sons are an asset to their church and outreach program. Chief McGee, a loved leader of the Creeks, was a close ancestor of Mrs. Gehman.

From way down south to way up north in Canada, we travel from the Creek Tribe to the Cree Tribe. Ron Favel and his wife Anita, who is from Oklahoma, pastor a church in Hodgsden, Manitoba. They have a beautiful sanctuary. Both of the Favels are graduates of the Northwest Indian Bible School.

My wife and I have been given names by the Indians. At Brainerd Indian School, the Bible students christened me Chief Hugs Himself because when I get tickled, I hug someone and generally it is myself. During a camp meeting at Athens, Michigan several years ago, Mrs. Elizabeth Sprague, a Chippewa and mother of Frances Montour, took Mrs. Gale and me into her Michigan tribe. The Chippewa of that area have the elderly women perform this act. I understand it is approved by their council. She drew a picture of floating clouds and then named my wife "Bethshalbam – Pretty Cloud." Her second name to be recognized was "Our O Gimma" meaning wife of Chief Leader. She then named me "Gezus" which means "Sun Rays." She illustrated this by showing sunshine on the clouds. She said that we belong together and have spread a lot of sunshine among her Indian people. As a second name I was given the name "Our Gimma," which means "Chief Leader." We responded by saying, We have many Indian friends from many tribes and we love them all.

Rev. Raymond Gowan arranged a tour of all the Indian reservations west of the Mississippi River. His wife and Mrs. Gale and I made the trip with him. Though I have never professed a call to the American Indian, they have become my first love in missions.

I wish to close this chapter by including some of the Sioux leaders of renown: Red Cloud, Spotted Tail, Sitting Bull, Crazy Horse, Red Shirt, Gaul, Rain in the Face, Crow King, American Horse, Little Wound, Bad Wound and Big Foot. All of these were chiefs except Sitting Bull who was a medicine man and a shrewd and powerful leader.

Indian Farewell

Chieftains, warriors, mothers, maidens, braves of the forest,
children of the plains;
yea, all tribesmen of the soil and bands of the earth;
hearken unto my words of farewell blessing:
Your journey may be but an arrow's flight or heap big for many moons.
Be it short or long, as you travel toward the setting sun,
be brave and strong.

May a good road rise to meet you;
may the path be easy upon your moccasins;
may the wind blow gently upon your back;
may the sun shine warm upon your face;
may the moon watch o'er your sleeps;
may the rain fall soft upon your lands;
and may the snows drive much meat to your camps.

Until we meet again, may the good Lord "cover you with His feathers"
and "hold thee securely in the hollow of His hand."
If our journey shall end before our paths cross again,
may we have so lived that we can meet in God's big tepee of heaven
and enjoy His blessing forever.

11

Happy Happenings

Miss Winnie Crouch

During my Bible School training, I had the privilege of taking some study courses with Miss Winnie Crouch as my instructor. She was a dear, loving saint of God. She took personal time to advise me how to maintain a steady walk with the Lord. This was at a time when the spiritual clouds were dark and discouraging. She taught Bible Doctrine in a manner that guided me into the Christian way of holy living.

Miss Crouch, in her own life, was a woman of deep piety. Her example of faith and devotion in prayer was a tremendous help to me. She tarried until she heard from heaven. This demonstrated a loving romance of faith with the Lord. This simple childlike trust is so essential in gaining answers from the Lord. Nothing thrills me more than an answer to prayer.

Miss Crouch introduced her students to books on simple faith such as: *Sammy Morris, Holy Ann, the Irish Saint* and *Praying Hyde,* the life of John Hyde. I read all three of these life stories frequently and they do stimulate my life of prayer. Examples of praying people mean much to me. Miss Crouch is high on this list.

In praying for divine leadership, in seeking for a special need, in intercession for a spiritual reviving of the Work, Miss Crouch led us in the prayer battle. This example has had much to do with building into my life a desire to see God perform miracles that truly honor Him. Let me testify that I am a miracle of redeeming grace as are all sinners who are saved by Jesus through His atoning blood.

What I wish to say is that Miss Winnie Crouch, as a Bible and Theology instructor, has been one of the HAPPIEST HAPPENINGS in my life. She was truly a "Mother in Israel." It is almost daily that I remember her for some reason: if it is only for her continual exhortation, "If we are going to just be 'nominal' Christians, there is no reason for us to exist."

I have written over one hundred HAPPY HAPPENINGS. I am preparing a book with that title. I am also including a few in this chapter. They have been meaningful to me. I trust they will be an encouragement to all of you. Do take your burden to the Lord. It is a HAPPY HAPPENING when God hears and answers our prayers. This chapter relates to a special area in my life.

Climbing to the Clouds

White, billowy clouds hung over the mountain range beyond. The four of us strained our eyes to the mountain terrain. Alice Omas was pointing and saying that her home barrio Latbang was just above the clouds on the crest of the mountain and her home was on the other side. It would take ten to eleven hours of fast walking for us slow hikers. It was early in the morning and we were already bathed in sweat.

The four of us were Bible Methodists. Alice, a beautiful maiden of 23, was our guide. Rev. Lauro Forto, our National President nearing the forty mark, was laboring with some physical handicaps. Rev. Rolando Lopez, in his early thirties, was the best hiker of the bunch. I was the only American and my 210 pounds and the nearly seventy years were both too high for the climb we were making.

On a previous trip we were in the Philippines when Mr. Marcos was deported and Mrs. Aquino became president. During the following trip we found the land in political turmoil with threats being made against both American military and civilians. As missionary secretary, I decided for the sake of our missionaries that we should take them from the country. They had already faced the guns of the New Peoples' Army (Communist Army). It was in this sad setting of bidding goodbye to our dear Philippine friends at the Bible College when we really came face to face with Alice Omas' burden for her people. She was then twenty years of age. I would like for you to meet Alice and hear her testimony.

Alice's tribe is Igorot. Her language is Dalangoya. This she grew up speaking. She spent grades three through six in another barrio where she learned to speak Ifugao and Ilocano dialects. In other institutes, she finished high school and learned to speak Tagolog and English, which are national languages. Her training and natural personality make her a very alert and attractive person.

She returned to her family to help make the living for her parents and brothers and sisters. There were spiritist worshipers in the area, but she was ignorant of the gospel. She gave her testimony to Mrs. Gale and me at our Bible College where she worked in the mission house for the Franklin Heers. Alice told me she had a deep longing in her heart to know about spiritual things. She told her parents that she believed there was a God and a heaven somewhere. There must be a way to go to heaven and she was going to leave and find the way. They felt they needed her help at home and wept when she left. She made her way down out of the mountains.

At Bayombong, the capital city of Nueva Viscaya, she met Felix and Sally, students from our Bible Methodist College. They helped her to get saved and she came with them and enrolled as a freshman. Her every effort, it seems, has been to learn the Christian way so that she can return to her people who were all pagans.

As we wept with our Filipino staff and students in the mission house, my wife and I turned to speak to Alice who was weeping broken heartedly. She fled to the bedroom and hid in the closet. When we found her, she came out in convulsions of sobbing. We tried to tell her we were not forgetting our pledge to her. With flowing tears she said, "You and our missionaries are leaving and my people will die in darkness." It was to a dear young lady weeping on my side that I pledged we would return to the Philippines and go with her to her people.

We already had climbed for a day to fulfill that pledge. The clouds drifted and returned and drifted away again before we finally reached Latbang. The people saw us coming in the distance. Someone said, "That must be them for they walk like children." Children take short steps and walk slowly when tired. The clouds lifted, but we found other clouds. Clouds of suspicion. They told me I was the first white person who had ever come to their barrio. I was the first American missionary they had ever seen. Most had not seen a white person before. They kindly received us, but there were clouds to obscure my purpose in coming. There were misty clouds of questions as to what message I was bringing. Why did this little company walk so far and climb so high? Oh, I wished I could tell them of the many nights I had prayed and asked God to help me to come to them with the message. For sixteen years we had prayed for the Igorot people. Since meeting Alice, it had been a daily prayer.

In our first service that night, the many clouds seemed to disappear. My three fellow-travelers, Alice Omas, Rev. Forto and Rev. Lopez blended in song with beautiful harmony. Alice's vibrant testimony brought us close together. Rev. Forto and Rev. Lopez alternated interpreting the messages which came deep out of my heart. They wanted us to speak more that first service. Alice told them of our weariness and pled for them to let us rest and we would let them ask questions at the close of the next service. I could not count the hands that were raised for prayer.

Time and space does not permit my telling of our trip down the mountain to Alice's home and meeting her people. It was a dangerous way to go and no laid out path to follow. I marveled, late the next night, how the people with pine knots, limbs and twigs, made that dangerous walk so late at night with those little flickering lights.

The second night brought people from far and near. What a precious service! The darkness hid the number of seekers. I do hope the Lord helped us to explain the way of salvation. Alice had felt the people would want to argue about the message and the truth of the gospel. The first question came from the barrio captain. They interpreted his question, "How soon can you send someone to tell us more and how soon can we build a church?" He further explained it would be two more years before Alice would graduate and return to them. They couldn't wait that long. Someone quickly answered, "Leave that to us, we'll furnish the land." Another called out; "We'll furnish the materials from the mountain forest."

We found at the top of the mountain, clouds that seemed to vanish. We found a mission field "WHITE UNTO HARVEST." The Igorots now have five churches and two daughter churches. Alice is now starting a new church in her home in the lowlands.

A Blue Corn Cookie

In our earlier years of contact with the Indians of the Southwest, we were invited to go with Clifford and Sheila Cheeseman to a place many miles beyond Shiprock. To reach our destination on time, we needed to leave in the wee hours of the morning. When it began to dawn, we could see the big shiprock stone. It certainly looked like a ship. It seems as though we were about an hour beyond when we came to a little church surrounded by a bleak, treeless, barren area. This was on the Navajo Indian Reservation.

When I got out to stretch, I saw an Indian lady walking. She had a baby on her back in a cradle board. One little one was held in her arms and two small children were hanging onto her large, flowing Navajo dress. I asked Mrs. Johnson, the Navajo lady interpreter, to help me talk with her. I learned she had gotten up early and walked ten miles with her little family to be there for the day.

I became speechless as she told how she got tired carrying the two and how the other two became so weary that they stopped and cried at times along the way. She then told the interpreter that she had heard me preach one other time before and wanted to hear me again. My heart was warmed and I felt a great compassion for this dear little Navajo mother.

Mrs. Cheeseman, the pastora, explained to the crowd who had now assembled that the church could not hold them all at one time. Those who could be in the first service must stay out and let others in for the afternoon service. There was no furniture in the church except a small pulpit stand and bench about four feet long.

All sat on the floor in about the same space as they stood. The full, flowing velvet-looking dresses took a lot of space. I was glad to see that the lady who had walked so far was able to get into the first service. One elderly couple had driven their horses and wagon 25 miles. When I finished preaching, three ladies knelt at the altar and that filled the bench. I then asked them all to kneel where they were. There was much weeping and praying as they knelt together.

After the service, a meal was served. I had asked Mrs. Cheeseman to leave out some of the mutton tallow from the stew. When the Indian ladies saw that she had left it out, they put it all back in. As we waited for dinner, the lady with four children came to me again. She felt the Lord had met her need. Mrs. Johnson again interpreted. The lady said she had one ear of blue corn. She had gotten up after midnight. First she shelled the corn; then pounded it to powder between rocks. She had made me a corn cake. It was a pretty blue color and shaped much like a big cookie.

When they brought me a bowl of stew, I was glad I was alone. Each family dipped their fry bread and ate from the same bowl. We were with the Salt Clan of the Navajos. They should be called the "Saltless Clan" since they use no salt. I sat on the ground with my legs crossed. The lady who had given me the corn cake sat down in front of me to watch me eat. I tried to smile with that saltless tallow sticking to the roof of my mouth. The little corn cake was nearly tasteless, but even if you were a million-aire you would appreciate a love gift.

This lady's sacrificial gift, the only ear of corn she had, was baked for me. Her long walk, carrying two and helping two others, was a sacrificial love gift. With the smile of Jesus on her face, it helped me eat every bite. Though the tallow in the stew did not taste good and the corn cake was tasteless, I still thank God for His countless blessings.

The giver of the precious gift could not come to the afternoon service. Later I saw her head back the ten miles with her baby on her back, one in her arms and two walking beside her. It would be late in the night when she got home. The little corn cake amply rewarded my coming. Learning of Jesus the Savior amply rewarded her coming.

They Curious; You Care

When speaking in a convention in Michigan, I met Robert and Betty Truesdale. They told me they had done missionary work among the Cree Indians at Hobema, Alberta, Canada. That was many moons ago. The fact that they had worked with Indians made a bond that drew us together. We have been in their home on various occasions and our conversations seemed always to lead to discussions of Indian tribes and individual Indian friends.

As a result of these visits, we decided to go together to Hobema, Alberta to where they had labored. At the time, we Gales were working with the Northwest Indian Bible School at Alberton, Montana. The Truesdales came for us at the school. We traveled in two different vehicles across the Flathead Indian Reservation. Since my wife and I were pulling a small travel trailer, we separated near the entrance of Glacier National Park. Truesdales went through the park and we took the main route around the southern edge. We got together again near Browning, Montana.

After traveling over 200 miles into Canada, and nearing the city of Red Deer, our car started over-heating. I foolishly tried to take the radiator cap off. The pressure was so great when I got it loose that it blew high into the air. The water and steam scalded my hands and face and much of my body. I was taken to a nearby hospital. With Canada's health system there was no cost to us. The doctor felt I should stay in the hospital overnight. He said the shock might be too great for my system. Foolishly, I decided not to stay. During the night I felt as though I were losing my mind. We spent the night in our little camper trailer. We had scheduled a service at Edmonton with the Free Methodists, so we separated, and the Truesdales stayed at Hobema with their Indian friends.

After our service, we returned to Hobema. We never saw a people show greater love to anyone than these Cree Indian friends did to the Truesdales. We Gales left to visit other reserves while Bob and Betty remained at Hobema. We learned that three of the reserves we visited had no church of any kind nor did they know of Jesus and salvation. We were given such a kind welcome that it was hard for us to leave.

Our two families joined again at Banff, which is the name of both a city and a national park in the beautiful Canadian Rockies. Bob Truesdale felt we needed to ride the chair lift to get a proper view of the magnificent sights. From our seats in the bubble-type chair cars, we could see where the glaciers were formed. This breathtaking scenery exceeded anything we had seen in the States.

At the top of the mountain was a gift shop. As we entered, we found ourselves in the midst of a large group of people who were gazing at an elderly buckskin-clad Indian. I took notice of his eagle feather war bonnet. I stood there wondering if he were an hereditary or an elected chief. As I looked intently at him, I wondered what tribe he represented. As I stood gazing with my mouth open, he suddenly pointed at me and motioned for me to come to him. It startled me, but I made my way over to where he stood. He said, "We have coffee." Pointing at the crowd, he remarked, "They curious; but you care." I asked if my wife and daughter could come, too. He replied, "Yes!"

As we had coffee, he told us his name was Tom Kaquits. He was chief of the Stony Indians. He shared with us his concern for his tribe. His own sons used liquor and were not worthy to become chiefs. He welcomed our praying with him. Later two of his granddaughters attended Northwest Indian Bible School.

This trip with the Truesdales was one never to be forgotten. In speaking of this time with the Truesdale family, I tell my friends, "You can get me to go to some enjoyable places if you do like they did. They paid all of our expenses!" It was truly a HAPPY HAPPENING to go with our Michigan friends to Indian Country and see the beautiful Canadian Rockies.

Chapter 12
Missions and Mission Schools
BRAINERD INDIAN SCHOOL

*I*n the beginning of Brainerd Indian School, Rev. John Kearns felt it was a priority to let the Indian people know that a white missionary had died in his effort to bring the gospel to them. His death was a result of exposure to harsh weather and from a desperate dedicated life of intercessory prayer for them.

During 1745-1746, David Brainerd ministered to Indians near Trenton, New Jersey. Here he was amazed at their immediate response to the Christian message.

Evangelist H. Robb French related the following: "David Brainerd, late in his young life, became consumptive. They could follow his trail in the snow as he spit blood along the way. On one occasion the heat from his body melted the snow out at arm's length as he knelt and so long and earnestly prayed."

By the fall of 1746, Brainerd was increasingly coughing up blood. The famous minister Jonathan Edwards brought him to his home at Northampton, Maine. There he died of tuberculosis on October 9, 1747.

Jonathan Edwards watched over David Brainerd all those months while he was slowly dying. Rev. Edwards said, "I praise God that it was in His providence that he should die at my house, that I might hear his prayers, that I might witness his consecration and that I might be inspired by his great example."

Jerusa, Jonathan Edwards' daughter, was in love with David Brainerd. He was such a holy man and she knew his time to live was limited. In those last days and hours of his life, she stood by him and lovingly and tenderly did what she could to relieve his fever and pain. Her father heard David Brainerd say to Jerusa, "If it were not for the life beyond the grave, I do not know how I could part from you." About six months after Brainerd died, Jerusa contracted tuberculosis. This seven-teen-year-old girl followed in death the one she had so dearly loved.

David Brainerd's journal shows how, with all consuming love for souls, he prayed down upon those helpless souls in heathen darkness, a veritable Pentecost. When William Cary read the life story of David Brainerd, he was so moved by it that he went to India. Henry Marten read his life story and with great compassion also went to India.

Payson read it as a young man. He was never so touched as by Brainerd's life. Robert Murray McCheyne read it and from his knees shook Scotland. Robert Moffat read it and later David Livingstone. They were so moved that they each gave their lives for Africa.

Jim Elliot, a twentieth century missionary, was so stirred by Brainerd's life that he gave his life for the Auca Indians. Dr. A.J. Gordon writes, "The great revival of the nineteenth century is due more to the prayer and consecration of David Brainerd than to that of any other man." He further wrote, "When Jonathan Edwards wrote that great appeal to Christendom to unite in prayer for the conversion of the world, which has been the trumpet call of modern missions, it was undoubtedly inspired by this dying man."

The life of David Brainerd so affected us who had part in the founding of the Brainerd Indian School that we felt we wanted our school to bear his name so we could tell our Indian friends that a white man loved them so much that he poured out his life for them here in our land and died at the young age of 29.

The Brainerd Indian School was located about 10 miles southwest of Hot Springs, South Dakota. We purchased a quarter section of land from Uncle Willie Fargo, as we lovingly called him. The campus had a flat valley where the gentle breezes blew.

This part of a chapter could easily become a whole book. I'll have to pick and choose. Many Indian families wanted their young people to have a Christian education. One year we had to turn away 310 young people for lack of room. The boys' dormitory was full; sleeping four boys to a bunk. The girls' dormitory, likewise, was filled to capacity. Every available space was taken. Even in our upstairs (one big room) we put down mattresses for girls. Meal time resembled George Mueller's orphanages. It became a daily financial burden, but God supplied our needs.

Most of the buildings that we had were moved in from a military base. It was very expensive to heat them. We trucked coal from Wyodak mine (named for Wyoming and South Dakota) located near Gillette, Wyoming. This amounted to a 300 mile round-trip. This was a soft coal which burned rapidly. We sometimes wondered if the supply would run out, but Wyoming has gigantic amounts of coal. In fact, for many years now, it has shipped as many as 30 trains a day; each pulling 110 cars loaded with 30 ton per car. One coal vein was 70 feet deep.

Mr. Paul Gilmore converted our coal furnaces into sawdust burners. This saved us lots of money. There was a sawmill about one-half mile from Brainerd School. That sawmill closed down and it wasn't long until the mountain of sawdust was gone. We started trucking it from a sawmill near Custer, South Dakota, an 80 mile round trip haul. Then a coal mine began using sawdust from the same mill. It was too much for them to supply both of us.

I had the staff pray with me to know what we should do. I felt impressed that the Lord wanted us to change to a propane gas system. I told the men they would all need to work overtime to get the buildings ready. Floor furnaces were the most reasonable priced and most easily installed.

I called Johnny Hagen and told him what we were doing and that we would need three large propane gas tanks to handle the campus. He quoted prices that sounded good to me. He said it would take two weeks for delivery. I said, "That's all right, it will take that long to pray in the money."

Early one morning I was praying for funds for the tanks. I spoke to the Lord, "We need money for three gas tanks." I felt He was saying, "You buy one and I'll give you money for the other two." I did something I had never done before. I laughed before the Lord and said, "You'll have to give money for mine, too, Lord." That was my heart agreement with my wonderful Lord. Two weeks went by quickly. I thanked God every day for the assurance He gave me.

One day while I was in the office, the phone rang, and Mrs. Gerow, the secretary-treasurer, handed it to me and said, "This is a call for you.

It's from Johnny Hagen." He said, "Reverend, your propane tanks came in this morning. I'll be bringing them out after four o'clock this afternoon." I replied, "Thanks, Johnny." I dropped to my knees and sweet assurance came. I went out to get the mail myself. I had to wait a while for the mail lady to come. She sort of teased me about coming after the mail myself.

One of the first letters was a personal one for me. I opened it quickly. It contained a check for the exact amount needed to pay for my tank. I praised the Lord and started sorting through the other mail. The mail carrier was our neighbor. She waited and watched me. There was most always lots of mail for Brainerd. Near the bottom of the stack, I found a letter addressed to me and also to the school. I opened it. A check inside was made out to the school for a bit more than the price of the other two tanks. I cried and praised God and so did Mrs. Buzz Hall. She said, "Isn't God good?" That was an understatement! I agree with what Rev. H. Robb French often said, "It's better to have a promise from God than to have a bank account."

This happening really affected us men. When the buildings were ready, nearly every furnace we needed (either from gifts or reasonable priced purchases) was on hand.

One day two of our men, Gordon Wills and Glen Case, came to me saying, "Did you know there are a few of the staff ladies who don't go along with this change – over to propane gas?" Then they told me that Miss Minnie Knect was the main one to object. They said, "She is afraid we will get it all installed and then will be unable to pay the gas bills." So I began listening when she prayed in the services: "Lord, help dear Brother Gale. All this strain is becoming too much for him." I went to talk with her. She was a saint to be revered. All of us had great respect for her.

I asked her, "Miss Knect, do I make your work hard for you?" She said, "Of course not, why do you ask?" My reply was, "I am beginning to feel you're not just praying for me, but at me." She kindly said, "I know what you mean. I have been greatly troubled over this change to propane gas." I told her to please keep praying for me. I intimated that God might show her this was His work! She took it like the saint she was.

We had all the furnaces installed except for the girls' dorm. I was coming out of the office one morning on my way to the barn to milk the cows. The weather had turned unseasonably cold for that time of year.

The girls who were to help prepare breakfast were running from the dorm to the kitchen. They were cold and expressing it by screaming. I spent much of the next night praying for a furnace for their dorm. The same thing happened the next morning. The girls screamed and ran for the kitchen, pulling up their coat collars.

The next night I got desperate as I prayed, "Dear Lord, You know as well as I do that we need this last furnace." Then I got an idea. I wanted to show the Lord I was trusting Him. I got my framing square and a pencil. I fumbled with my keys until I found the one for the girls' dorm. I opened the door and turned on the light. From the arrangement of the nails on the floor, I located the floor joists. I thought perhaps I should have measured another furnace, but then I prayed silently, "Lord, I am going to mark this area for the furnace and trust you to fit it to the hole." I measured and marked the floor. When I stood up, it looked good to me.

If you ever try something like this, you can depend on it, the devil will tantalize you severely. I got down inside that rectangular marking and prayed until I felt peace in my heart. I went early the next morning and told Gordon and Glen that I wanted them to cut the hole for the furnace and box it in. They both asked, "Do you have the furnace?" I answered, "No, but I am trusting God for the right furnace." One of them said, "We would be more certain if we had the furnace first!" I said, "Go ahead and cut it." They smiled as much as to say, "You're the boss."

The next morning early I was dressed in my overalls and shirt that showed marks of the dairy barn. I was still on the steps of the office, when a man drove up in a pickup. He got out and came over to where I was standing. He asked, "Who is the 'head honcho' around here?" I replied, "Dressed in this kind of garb, it would be difficult to accept, but I am the president of this school." He went on to tell me he was our neighbor. He was going to work in Hot Springs and from the gravel highway had seen my office light. He was hoping somebody would be up. He continued, "I said to my wife while eating breakfast, 'I have never stopped at that Indian school. I'm going a little early to see if I can talk to someone.'" He went on to say, "When I went out to my garage, my eyes fell upon a new floor furnace I had bought. I put it in the back of my pickup. It is still in the crate. Can you use a propane gas floor furnace?"

I looked in the direction he was pointing and there stood Miss Knect. I wondered why she was out so early. I exclaimed excitedly to the

102

neighbor, "Yes, we surely can! Just back up to the next building. That is the girls' dormitory. I want to get the two men who cut the hole for the furnace." Startled, the neighbor exclaimed, "They did what?" I replied, "I prayed for a furnace and had them cut the hole so we would be ready for it."

Miss Knect came over. The men uncrated the furnace. They had used hand saws and I noticed they had cut inside the lines a little. If they had kept right on them, they would not have had to push to get it in place. The Lord had it delivered to the dorm and it fit on all four sides! Miss Knect hurried to me. "Seeing what God did for you, Brother Gale, I'll be happy to follow your leadership. God is with you," she exclaimed.

I would like to pause in my writing to brag a little! First, I want to tell you that I am very simple. I have taken a lot of schooling. I had to train to get on in life. But I want to brag about Jesus who saved me. When He did, I found Him to be a miracle-working Savior. I love Him with all my heart!

We had received official advice to drill another well at Brainerd Indian School. The only funds we could come up with was money allocated to finish our metal Quonset gymnasium. I borrowed from that fund so we would have money for the new well. I went to the bank and personally took out a loan for $1,500.00 to replace what we had borrowed.

I asked the Lord if He would send funds so I could pay it back. If I remember correctly, I had them divide it into 12 payments, plus the interest. Some the money to meet these payments came in early. Each was from a different source. A few times the money arrived on the exact due date. I never made a late payment. There is a price to pay in prayer. God has no money for large offerings in answer to ten cent prayers. He wants us to love and trust Him.

Brainerd Indian School is no longer operating, but its memories live on. The Cascade Stream heads up at Keith Park where several springs originate about a mile below the school campus and tumble over the Cascade Falls.

Many students made their start for God on these grounds. Greater than the financial and healing miracles are those students who were converted and made their start toward heaven.

The stone quarry above the campus; the big 12,000 gallon tank where the water by hydraulic pressure was kept full to irrigate the campus; where the REA System lighted the campus; where the entrance rock said, "Without a Vision the People Perish"; where the exit sign said, "Come Again." This was Brainerd Indian School: The Home of the Warriors and Braves! Where Friday night was reserved for fun and games and Sunday for worship! God bless you! COME AGAIN!

NORTHWEST INDIAN BIBLE SCHOOL

In 1968 the Brainerd Indian School staff came to the decision that we must move. There were circumstances related to the merger of the Wesleyan Methodist and Pilgrim Holiness Churches that prompted this unanimous action. It was decided that since Rev. Robert Pelton was the president, Merle Rough head of maintenance and chief builder and Rev. William Gale, former president and one of the original founders, we three should constitute a search committee.

There was a Free Methodist School at Wessington Springs, South Dakota that was closing and was for sale. It would have cared for all of our needs. The buildings were in good repair and the price was low for its value. The City Council voted to pay a good share of that price if we would accept the offer. After prayer and special consideration, it seemed it would not be fair to the merging church who would need to replace the staff. We would likely be in competition over the Indian people since we would be located in the same state as the Brainerd Indian School. We determined to show a Christ-like spirit.

The story of the Nez Perce Indian Lament and the fact that there was no Protestant Christian school for training Indians in that vast area of the northwest, was a challenge to us men of the committee. In our search we came to the Bitter Root Valley in Montana. This was far to the west and just beyond the Continental Divide in the Rocky Mountains. It was very close to the Flathead Reservation. We searched many properties. One that was on the Flathead Reservation was a ranch with some very good buildings, all usable. It had a stream that flowed through the heart of the land. It was breathtaking to see. Robert Pelton and Merle Rough got a big laugh at my expense when I asked the realtor, "What's on that land be of?" I meant to say above. When they showed the large farm house, we entered by the side door. When we entered, Rev. Pelton said, "What a huge chicken!" He meant to say kitchen. We had another hearty embarrassed laugh. I guess it wasn't our day. When we tried to introduce ourselves, Rev. Pelton and I started about the same time. I said, "I'm Gale." I think Rev. Pelton meant to introduce me when I spoke up. He then said, "I'm Pale." We all lost it and went into fits of laughter. We would rather have you laugh with us than at us. Those people had a hard time understanding our amusement.

To hurry this part of the search account, the property was named GLORY BE RANCH. We learned that the sale was so high, it took all of the glory out of it and we had to let it be. Reverend and Mrs. Dallas Wadsworth royally entertained us in their home at Hamilton, Montana. They were dear friends to all of us.

One of the properties we looked at was located west of Missoula, Montana and across the Clark Fork River from the small town of Alberton. The first time we looked at it we felt it was too large a parcel of land. We continued our search. The other two men thought we should go back and look at the land near Alberton again. We drove a ways onto the land. The road made a turn and we followed it a short distance when Rev. Pelton said to Merle Rough, "Stop here." We all got out and stepped over to a spot nearby. We knelt in prayer, facing each other. God came and met us as we prayed. Together we said, "This is the place." The whole plot was nearly a half section of land. The price was far less than most properties we had looked at which were much smaller. We had looked at a few which were smaller and less expensive but were for various reasons not suitable.

Soon after we arranged the purchase we contacted a well driller as one of our first projects. The school staff was completing their last year at Brainerd. We Gales were the first to move out. We parked our small travel trailer in Alberton. I was alone with the well driller. I took him back on a mountain drive where he could overlook the undeveloped campus. As we came down, we arrived at the place near the front road. The driller said, "Reverend Gale, stop here." We got out and he led the way to where we three men had prayed and decided that this was the right property. The well driller pointed at the very same location and said, "This is the spot." I asked why. His reply was, "I can't give you a good earthly reason, but feel we'll get a good well here."

We employed him to drill the well. It was about this time when Merle and Martha Rough moved out to help us. When the driller told me the well was ready, I asked, "How much water will it pump?" He smiled and said, "I don't know. I have pumped it hard and continuously for two days and it measures the same level. It should care for a small city." The water tested a little hard, but was classified as a soft water well in that area. This was one of the miracles at NIBS.

Reverend and Mrs. Lester Bennet felt the Lord leading them to come out to help with the building of the houses. Soon after the Bennets, Reverend and Mrs. Bennie Veeder also felt led to help with the building work. Merle Rough and these men and all the recruits we could get worked hard to get the housing ready for the staff.

When we first moved to the land, we found it occupied by many wild animals. There were deer and elk in numbers. We would see them early in the day and late in the evening. Every day we saw mountain sheep come to water at the spring above Alberton. The black bear upset our garbage cans at night. Our nearest neighbor to the west killed 17 bears (one a grizzly) the year we moved out there. James Feracioly killed a mountain lion near our land. We often saw their tracks in the snow. The animals tend to move back when man moves in.

There are some events which were miraculous. Mrs. Gale and I drew a plot showing the large acreage. We traveled to many churches and told many people of the land project. We colored in the acres as the money came in. It was a huge project, but the Lord helped us to raise the funds for all of the acres and for the first ten houses during the first year. The Robert Houses, friends who owned the Conner Lumber Company, sold us lumber for less than they sold to lumber yards. Thanks to these dear friends.

We tried to get credit for the project, but had nothing of value to show in the area. Someone told us Montana Mercantile Company had the largest supply of building materials in the area. We prayed about it and Merle and I went in to see if they would accept us. The day before we had built an outdoor toilet and that was the only building we owned. I suggested that Merle tell them about our buildings and I would show them my many credit cards. We couldn't help but laugh when we thought what little we had to impress them.

The office building was large with aisles running between the individual offices. The partitions were low and we could see into the offices as we walked by. We were able to talk with a credit manager. He came from one of the more secluded offices. We told him of the school, the land and of our plans to build. He thanked us for coming in, but explained that they only sold to lumber yards and hardwares. Their policy was to protect these businesses. We tried to persuade him by telling him of the amount we would be building. He still held firm.

Then I asked him if he were the top man. He said, "No there is one man over me." I asked him if he would be offended if we talked to him. He said, "I'll go and see him for you." We didn't want him to do that because we knew how he felt. Merle and I bowed our heads and quietly prayed. He was only gone a short time and came back smiling. He said, "We're going to set you up." We looked at him questioning. Then he said, "We've checked on both of you at Hot Springs, South Dakota. You have very high ratings with the bank. We learned enough to tell you that with us the sky is the limit. We have a man coming to show you around so you will know what you can get here. Here comes the man now." He walked away a few steps and then turned around and said, "By the way, if you need a credit reference, feel free to use us." As the man showed us all they handled, we felt almost as though we owned the place. On the way home we stopped at an automotive supply and used our new credit reference. We found that Montana Mercantile was a good friend to us as a reference for wholesale buying.

Early in our project and before the staff moved to Montana, Roughs, Bennets, Veeders and us Gales met Sundays for worship. The Allegheny Mission leaders thought we should hire the footers and water lines to be dug commercially. During Saturday night we had a time of prayer. I was troubled about that cost. I mentioned my burden to the others. I said, "We are all Christian workers and perhaps need to pray more than being preached to." Then I explained how I felt we needed a tractor. Merle and I had made two trips hunting for one. As a group, we decided to pray for the exact need. Merle reminded us that at Brainerd we had a John Deere 440 and it was a small crawler. The John Deere 1010 was a later model and he thought one mounted on rubber would be better with which to get around. One of the other men said, "We will need a front-end bucket type lift." I think I suggested a back-end loader for hauling dirt.

We took both morning and evening services to pray for a John Deere 1010 mounted on rubber with a front-end bucket lift and a back-end loader. We got a few other requests into our praying, but many times the group of us went over the particular tractor need. We all retired that night wondering how the Lord would work it out. All of us had been through spiritual storms and did love to pray. Praying so exact seemed new to all of us. The next morning Reverend Bennet went to Alberton to get the Missoulian paper. He came back driving fast. He told us there was an advertisement of a tractor for sale which was the exact description of the tractor for which we had been praying. He said he had a strange experience. As he started to dial the number, his hand trembled so he could hardly dial. When the man answered, he said, "Yes, I have the John Deere for sale, but how did you get my number? I have advertised it three times and each time they put in a wrong number. I haven't gotten a call. You must have dialed the wrong number." He told Reverend Bennet he would hold it for one hour and then it would go to the first buyer. We did not want to chance losing it, so we went right away into Missoula. When we came around a bend and saw it sitting near the road on the side of the hill, that yellow tractor looked like gold to me. I couldn't hold back the praise when I looked at a John Deere 1010 mounted on rubber with the front-end bucket lift and the back-end loader.

The man came out and started the tractor. He showed us that everything worked. We then asked his price. We had planned to discuss the price, but when he told us, I quickly told him if he would throw in the dump truck at that price, we would take it. He said he would do that and use the truck to deliver it to our campus. He would need it yet for about ten days before its delivery. I responded, "Good, we don't have the money and we'll need time to pray it in." The God who was good enough to answer our prayers certainly supplied the money to pay when the machine was delivered. The work done in one week with the John Deere would have cost us as much as the purchase price of the tractor if we had hired it done commercially. Merle Rough is gifted in many ways and it was not long until he had it running like a new one. Jim Feracioly told me when they sold the John Deere some years later, they got three times what they paid for it and they still had the truck.

After the staff moved out, the students came. We were more than busy. The moving truck became a classroom. We built a room on the back of our 50's trailer that had been purchased for our dwelling. That room was needed for an elementary classroom. Some classes were held in garages. The dining hall was at first located at Rough's trailer and later in the basement of the Pelton house. This just touches on the fringe edge of what was done in order to get the school into action. The degrees of our staff enabled us to be state accredited.

The building work and demands on the treasury were enormous. One incident I remember as though it were yesterday. We had gathered for a staff meeting. President Pelton came in with a manila folder in his hand. He began the meeting by telling us he had received the conference check to pay our bills, but we needed an additional $17,000.00. Those bills made the folder bulge. He continued, "I am going to pass these out and each of us are to pray for the funds needed to pay these bills. You are to pray in the funds for the bills I give you." Mine turned out to be from the first two places from which we had opened accounts. Montana Mercantile's bill was over $10,000.00. The other was not so large. This was not my first time to look at a big bill, but these looked huge to me. I felt so responsible that every bit of joy drained out of me. These were more than the rest were praying for individually. I think the enemy took advantage and spoke about my good credit rating. "What will friends at Montana Mercantile think of you now? What will the rest of the staff think? What will happen to Northwest Indian Bible School?" I can remember saying, "Lord, this is your work; we're doing it for You." It seemed as if a kind, loving hand was placed on my shoulder. It seemed the Lord was saying, "I'll not forsake you now." The healing balm of Calvary and the loving voice of the Lord is so precious in a time like this. Answers to prayer have sometimes come after weeks of praying. I want to magnify the Lord for His sweet assuring love.

It was at our next staff meeting when flood tides broke loose in my soul and in the souls of the rest of the staff. When Rev. Pelton stood before us, he said, "I want to show you how many of those $17,000.00 bills are left to be paid." He opened the folder and inverted it. Not one bill fell out; the folder was empty. What a time of rejoicing! Additionally, President Pelton said, "Don't ask me where the money came from, for God laid it on the hearts of many all over the country." These are not verbatim words but they do convey his message, I believe. As I write tears are flowing as I remember the deep love of a caring Lord. He loves the Indian; He loves His workmen. Let me continue this happy happening by saying "Let's all pray!"

When we as a staff decided to move to Montana, one of the major contributing factors was the account of the Nez Perce Indians seeking the Book of Life. My poem describes this:

The Nez Perce Lament

In eighteen hundred and thirty-one,
The Nez Perce in deliberation
Sent forth their mighty chiefs
In an assigned delegation.

They longed to gain the Bible
The White Man's Book of Life,
Hoping by its message
To be freed from sinful strife.

Four chiefs were chosen;
Sheer strength would not avail.
Two were young and two were old—
The way, an unmarked trail.

The Speaking Eagle, first old chief;
Man of the Morning, the latter;
No Horns on His Head, a younger
And Rabbit Skin Leggings, the other.

Long was their journey
And great was their need;
They finally reached St. Louis—
Alas! Not to succeed.

One heartbroken chief
Knowing why they went
Spoke his heart of sorrow
In the following lament.

"For many moons we traveled
With strong arms and hands,
From the setting sun
Through strange enemy lands.

"Our people afar have sent us
From the darkness of tepee hut.
I came with one eye open,
Go back with both eyes shut.

"You showed me your dancing women,
To my deep despair,
The Spirit with candles worshiped,
But the Book was not there."

"You showed us pictures of heaven,
Good lands beyond abound;
Nowhere in all you showed us
Was the Book of Heaven found."

"I hoped that I might carry
Much good back to my people."
By this he meant the Bible
And church with simple steeple.

"Now I am returning
With an empty token;
My moccasins hold tired feet,
Both my arms are broken."

No Horns on His Head, the speaker
No help was able to find,
Said, "How can I return
When both my eyes are blind?

We'll gather in Big Council
After one more snow,
None has come to tell us,
We have no Book to show.

"No word will then be spoken
By our warriors or old men.
One by one, go out in silence
And down the path of sin.

"My people will die in darkness,
Go to hunting grounds in vain;
No White Man will go with them,
No Book to make it plain."

He closed his oration saying,
"I have no more words."

Northwest Indian Bible School, sponsored by Allegheny Wesleyan Methodist Connection of Churches is located at Alberton, Montana. The campus is beautiful. It is staffed by excellent workers. They are to be commended for their outreach to the American Indian.

PHILIPPINE BIBLE METHODIST COLLEGE

In 1974 I was elected Mission Secretary for the Bible Methodist Church. This was a joy as well as a challenge to me. I was faced with a very important decision soon after I took office. Dr. Rufus Reisdorph contacted Reverend V.O. Agan to see if we would consider taking the Philippine Church as our mission field.

This work had been started by Reverend J.F. Simpson and the Dakota Conference of the Wesleyan Methodist Church. Reverend Romeo Baronia, the first president, had attended God's Bible School. He and Dr. Reisdorph and Rev. Simpson were schoolmates. Rev. S. J. McIntyre was treasurer of the Dakota Conference. He, too, had attended God's Bible School. These Wesleyan Methodist men all had a share in establishing the Philippine work. Rev. Simpson made numerous trips to the field. Rev. L.D. Harris went to build many wood-framed church buildings.

I was well acquainted with all of these men. We all had our background in the Dakota Conference. Along with being president, Rev. Simpson pastored the Strathaven Wesleyan Pioneer Church at Rapid City, South Dakota. I preached often for him when he traveled to the Philippines. Through these men, I was acquainted with the Philippine Mission Work. Dr. Robert Lytle was General Mission Secretary for the Wesleyan Methodist Church. By our mutual and personal acquaintance, we were able to work out an agreement that transferred the work to the Bible Methodist Church. There was also a small cash settlement given to us.

This has been a good work and is having growth. All of our pastors are graduates of our Bible Methodist College. While I was General Missions Secretary, I made 13 trips to the Philippines. Mrs. Gale was with me for 11 of these. Pages could be written about the Philippine Church and the Bible Methodist College.

The Republic of the Philippines is a third world country. World War II left it suffering wreckage and with a tremendous death toll. The USA became its deliverer. Men who were forced to march in the Bataan

Death March privately told stories that made me weak and sick. Such terrible treatment is not possible to put in writing.

Because we as a church have endeavored to put loving arms around them, some of the most lovable people on God's great planet earth have come forward to build a strong church. Rev. Louis Ordonez, second president of the Philippine Work, assisted by Jose Barbero and Lauro Forto, were the key leaders holding the churches and college together. All the pastors and pastoras, along with lay leaders from the churches, have been the backbone of the Philippine Church.

On our second Philippine trip, Rev. Ordonez took us to a new province where no white missionary had been. Since we had no mission vehicle at that time, we traveled the major portion of the journey by bus. Finally, we transferred to a jeepney and finished traveling by tricycle (Motorcycle with attached side-car).

The little church where I was to preach was usable, but lacked a good bit from being finished. It was just a short distance from the home where we were to spend the night. Rev. Ordonez introduced us to the family and then had to leave right away to go back to our Bible College to teach. The lady of the home was very hospitable. She knew we were weary so she showed us to the bamboo bed (a wooden frame covered with bamboo strips with a grass mat over it). We stretched out for our siesta. I was awakened and looked up to see the biggest rat I had ever seen. It was hanging over a rafter, showing its teeth. I thought it was going to jump down on me. My quick movement made it take off running down a ceiling joist. If it is still alive, I hope it is still running! They told me later that kind of rat is called a rice rat and is the best kind to eat.

After preaching service that evening, the family and friends gathered in for a big rice supper. All of the people who came for the meal stayed for the night. We went back to our bamboo bed. The room was full of ladies. We discovered that this room was to be their bedroom, also. Mrs. Gale whispered, "William, how am I going to get ready for bed?" I replied, "Get behind me." I spread out my coat and she hurried and slipped into bed. The ladies (about 20 in all) were waiting on me to go to bed so they could put their mats down.

I jokingly said, "This is a new experience for me: A bamboo bed, a bamboo house and now a mosquito net. How am I going to get ready for bed?" I wanted to say, "And this a ladies' dormitory, too." Just then two elderly ladies said, "Oh, we'll show you!" They came over to the bed. Each was carrying a little kerosene light. These lights don't give much light, but do make a lot of smoke. The last thing I needed was two ladies to help me into bed. My wife was enjoying my predicament and I thought maybe her laughter would shake the bed to pieces. One lady held up the side of the net and the other held the light so I could see to undress.

I took off my shoes to let them know that I could do the rest myself. But they nodded and stayed right there. I took off my shirt and nodded again. They smiled and nodded back. I dropped my trousers and jumped for the bed. They both reached in and pulled the covers over me and patted me good-night! The kerosene's light showed me a wall-to-wall people. There was no way to walk out in the night.

One of the ladies stayed with her husband in another room where the men slept. For some reason she wept and wept over some burden that broke her heart. As I listened, I thought, "Here in this home is a wall-to-wall people, but in this land is an ocean to ocean people who need to know our Savior."

We witnessed many events of a similar nature which broke our hearts and made us weep. This is Bible Methodist's day! Our day! A land of over 7,000 islands with at least a third inhabited. Our work is laid out for us.

Our Bible college is an answer to their spiritual need. I saw this as our Missionary Secretary Dr. Michael Avery saw it; as Rev. Gary Brugger saw it; as Rev. John Parker sees it. The Philippine Work needs our help. The Philippine missionaries, the Timothy Keeps and the David Blacks need our help. The Philippine leaders need our help. Many are hurting and need our help. "The night cometh when no man can work."

LATIN AMERICAN BIBLE INSTITUTE

The Bible Methodist Mission Board, due to visa problems, decided to relocate the institute in Mexico. The Mexican government passed some new laws that made this advantageous. There were other problems also that affected this decision, I am sure.

There had been three major reasons the mission board had earlier chosen to build on the States side. I wish to relate these since we witnessed so many miracles.

Edwin Tomes and I looked North and South in Mexico for property we felt would be a proper location. Acreage was much more costly in Mexico and materials for building more expensive than in our country. After many days of searching, we came back to the mission house at Weslaco, Texas. I prayed much for divine guidance. In the middle of the night, I saw clearly a metal Quonset building. I thought about it and remembered that Erwin Bourne had dismantled and moved such a building from Michigan to Donna, Texas for a camp meeting. I prayed for direction the next night and saw that Quonset building again. I prayed for the camp meeting. The third night I saw the same building. I thought then that I had better look into the situation. I found that the camp was closed and the building was for sale.

Two things had happened that seemed to be from the Lord. The night before we came back from Southern Mexico, I stayed in the home of Attorney Pedro Munoz. His wife spoke English so it was easier for them to entertain me. That night Pedro told me that we should not build in Oaxaca, Mexico. If we built a nice-looking property, the State or National Government would likely take it. He further said that Mexico has a greater North-South problem than we have in the States and that students would not come from the north to a school in the south. But, he said there is a clout about going across the border into the U.S.

Not knowing that Pedro had talked with me, Rev. Isaias Monoz (with Rev. Edwin Tomes interpreting) gave me several reasons why it would be better to build in the States. I'll not take time to enumerate them. They all seemed logical. With the two good Mexican brethren (an attorney and our own National Mexican Bible Methodist President) advising us to build State-side, we decided it would be best to follow their recommendations.

When I talked with Rev. Bourne, he said he would sell us his own living quarters and the small rental house for a reasonable figure. If we purchased these houses, the Quonset building and the acreage that went with them, we would have nearly 10 acres. Since it would be going for another holiness cause, their board would let us have it for a good price.

When we presented this package to our mission board, they unanimously felt this to be divine leadership. J.L. Collins had helped me in other Missions projects. When he found we were going to build, he prayed about coming to help. He said to his wife, "Do you know what I feel the Lord wants us to do?" She replied, "I think the Lord wants us to go and help Brother Gale build that school."

They were God's answer to our project. On the campus was a large two-story house. The second story furnished living quarters for the school president and the first story was all furnished for entertaining those who came to help build.

No group will give more sacrificially than Bible Methodists when they are challenged. In less than two years we had a half million dollar property. The campus consisted of two houses, a trailer home, large Quonset gymnasium with a cement block entry area including modern bath and showers for both men and women. On the far end was the Olive Scott Music Center with a choir area and four piano training rooms.

Also there was a three-car garage for teaching drivers' education and to house the school vehicles; two-story dormitories for ladies and men; a kitchen-dining area with cook's residence over the kitchen; a classroom building with a library addition on one end and educational office on the other. These were all beautiful buildings. Since I do architectural and blue print layouts, we were able to save these expenses.

It had finally come down to the last week when the final funds came in and we were able to dedicate our campus debt-free. Dr. Michael Avery made the financial report. We received our tax-free number (74-251-3578). Ben H. Branch wrote that a license was not needed for our type of school. Our Certificate of Incorporation was recognized on April 26, 1988. Dr. John Shimmer, Regional Director for the Association of Christian Schools International, came personally to the dedication with a letter which stated that the Latin American Bible Institute had been given approval and recognition by their institution. This all made it possible for Mr. Omer G. Sewell to declare that students from all Spanish-speaking countries could obtain visas to go to our school. Striking the podium, he said triumphantly, "And I signed this letter MYSELF!"

Those attending the dedication service will well remember how we Bible Methodists shouted and praised the Lord.

13

Life of Travels

ALASKA — Our Forty-ninth State

We developed a special friendship with Rev. John and Yvonne Betters. They were pastoring the First Wesleyan Methodist Church in Kansas City, Kansas. We talked about taking a trip somewhere together. Both families had a strong desire to go to Alaska, so that was what we decided to do. I said to Rev. Betters, "You need to sign a pledge so you won't back out."

After planning the trip, we moved to Alberton, Montana to raise funds to help establish Northwest Indian Bible School. I felt overwhelmed. I needed time and funds. When I called Rev. Betters to tell him I wouldn't be able to go, his reply was, "I wonder who should have signed a pledge!" We went to Alaska. I'm a man of my word.

The Betters got books to study and saw a film on Alaska which even highlighted the mile posts along the way. My wife and I had a lot to learn. We did know that the Alcan Highway would not be a super highway! As we traveled through Canada, we were privileged to visit a number of Indian reserves. We had a great time cooking out and tenting along the way. When we arrived at Fairbanks, Alaska, we were welcomed into the home of our long-time friends, Gladys Main and Ida Merrill.

The Betters came home with a burden for Alaska. They resigned their church and returned to establish the Far North Missionary Fellowship. The Betters have been faithful in giving the gospel message across these years. We could write a book about this trip, but we wish to write of other journeys, so will need to travel on. But we declare that this was an unforgettable experience with a couple of God's finest missionaries.

BOLIVIA — Home of the Enyarts

The Enyart family was a missionary family in Bolivia. Rev. Joseph Enyart was born there. When I was teaching at Union Bible College at

Westfield, Indiana, he invited me to go with him to speak for some services in the country of his birth.

The airport at La Paz is 12,786 feet in elevation. It is the highest major airport in the world. Many travelers require oxygen when arriving. I felt short of breath when walking upgrade, but got by without oxygen.

The James McBryant family were the missionaries for the Friends Church in the highlands. We did not go to the Lowlands area. James told me the Aymara Indians knew about me because I had worked among the Indians in the States. They had made requests for me to preach for them. Since Rev. Enyart had furnished my ticket, I needed to reserve my time for them. They agreed to my preaching some for some other groups.

Rev. James Fulton had told me that there were many Quakers in Bolivia. Six of these groups had their background with Union Bible College. Most of the ladies from these Aymara tribes wore derby-looking hats and dresses with very full skirts.

Rev. McBryant had asked me to speak for the first service with the Aymara Indians, but I felt I had not yet adjusted to the high elevation enough to preach. He consented to speak to the congregation which numbered over 3,500 by head count. As he was preaching, he became very ill and had to leave the tabernacle. The missionary asked me to take over. Since the sermon had been delivered in Spanish and then inter-preted into the Indian language, I was at a loss as to what had been preached. I was relieved when the missionary asked me to give my testi-mony. I had to speak through Spanish and Aymara interpreters. At the close of the service, the congregation clapped and then it turned into a moving altar service.

During the next meeting with the Aymaras, the congregation numbered over 7,000. (They take a head count for each of their services.) They have three camps with a total of over 20,000. They asked if I would be willing to become their new leader. They had prayed for an older man to come and felt I would be the one. I told them I would not be able to, but appreciated their invitation.

At the meeting with the Quaker group to whom I had originally come to speak, over 1,000 attended. I spoke to the missionaries the last days I was in Bolivia. What a wonderful trip!

ENGLAND

Methodism was born in England. Wesley was the founder. Robert and Bonnie Thompson and we Gales made this trip together. We stayed at Alma Mansion on the Pillar of Fire Campus. Rev. Bernard Dawson had the oversight of the work and pastored the church. Rev. Lenny Mancino took us to many places in the country. He did a super job. I don't think anyone could have done better at showing us the places we had on our list.

We saw Bristol, the home of the Wesleys. Their home and the chapel are preserved as they were in the days of Samuel and Susanna, the father and mother of John and Charles. Their home in London has been modernized. Wesley's roots were first on our list.

Cliff College, in Bristol, is now located in the buildings where George Mueller's Orphanage was housed. These are unbelievable structures!

Trafalgar Square in downtown London is a famous landmark. Westminster Abbey, like St. Paul's Cathedral, is one of the largest churches in England and is one of London's oldest and best known churches. David Livingstone and many famous people are buried there. When we visited the church, they were having a service and a guard told me I couldn't enter. Just as he told me, others came and cut the ribbons. The people went out the side doors and I rushed to the front and stopped. I wondered how to find David Livingstone's grave. The names of those who are buried there are engraved in the floor. I started to read some of the names. I looked down and I was providentially standing right on the space where his name was engraved.

I had to ask the Lord to help me. I started to weep and knelt because Livingstone's life had affected my life so much. I had a sweet time of prayer.

Charles Haddon Spurgeon pastored the Metropolitan Tabernacle, which seated 6,000. Spurgeon was one of Britain's greatest preachers. He was called the "Prince of Preachers."

We were thrilled to see Big Ben Clock located in a down-town tower. We could set our watches by it, for it is known to keep perfect time. The chimes sounded out melodious and clear.

In England they drive on the left side of the road. It would be hard for us to adjust to this. We were impressed by London's great subway system, by the Thames River separating the major parts of the city and by the famous London Bridge.

The "Changing of the Guard" at Buckingham Palace was a sight long to be remembered. We witnessed Queen Elizabeth riding a horse in the lead group. We thoroughly enjoyed seeing the guards with special matching costumes riding on beautiful arch-necked horses performing for the ceremony. Buckingham Palace where the queen lives was an impressive sight.

Twenty-one miles west of London we visited Windsor Castle, a magnificent structure. Touring the building and reading of some of their early kings, we were reminded that England had a very corrupt history. This makes one marvel at the Wesleyan revival that swept across the British Isles and also reached our fair land. Like our own country, England is in need of revival again.

ISRAEL

It was my privilege to make three trips to Israel. Mrs. Gale was with me the first two times. Rev. Harold Schmul and I were together the third time. My mission students from Union Bible College at Westfield, Indiana, along with Rev. Raymond Crooks and friends from the Church of God Holiness, made up our group the second trip. Rev. Robert Thompson sponsored the first and third journeys.

It is always a highlight to be in Israel. In measuring the land area, it is north to south "from Dan to Beersheba" and east to west "from the Jordan River to the Mediterranean Sea." We visited many interesting and meaningful sights. To actually walk and travel where Jesus had walked made the Bible really come alive.

BETHLEHEM was very special to all of us. We saw it from the area of the Shepherds' Caves. It was late in the evening and the lights began to come on. Someone in our group started singing "O Little Town of Bethlehem." We all joined in and a tingling feeling went up and down my spine and goose pimples all over my being. I could almost hear the baby "coo"! We were looking down upon the birth place of our lord.

JERICHO is a major city in Israel. It is called the City of Palms. It is located 5 miles west of the Jordan River, 7 miles north of the Dead Sea and 15 miles northeast of Jerusalem. It is 800 feet below sea level while Jerusalem is 400 feet above sea level. From Jericho to Jerusalem, you would ascend over ½ mile in 15 miles. We were surprised to learn that some of the priests walked this distance. This city is the oldest city in the world. It is an oasis with a tropical climate. On our first trip we learned of three Jerichos. We saw the ruins of Old Testament Jericho. New Testament Jericho had been uncovered by archaeologists by the time we toured Israel the third time. We all enjoyed being in modern Jericho.

THE DEAD SEA is 47 miles long, 10 miles wide and is 1,300 feet below sea level. It has no outlet and the salt concentration is 4 times that of the ocean water. Modern Sodom has been built along the west shore of this sea. Our tour bus took us into the rebuilt city. We were embarrassed at what we saw. Men were swimming without a stitch of clothing; women were wearing very suggestive swimwear. We had brought our lunch so found a secluded place to eat. We wondered what we would do if the Lord came and found us in Sodom. Archeologists have not yet discovered Gomorrah.

While we were by the Dead Sea, we took a chair lift to MASADA, the Roman rock fortress built by Herod. Jewish Zealots seized the fortress in 66 A.D. The Roman armies laid siege to Masada seven years later and more than 900 Zealots committed suicide rather than fall into Roman hands. Seeing these ruins and hearing the story made a sad, sensational experience.

A bit over a century ago, Mr. Gordon came to Israel from England. Looking from his hotel window, he saw a dome shaped rock just outside the city of Jerusalem. He exclaimed, "That has to be GOLGOTHA." He learned that the land was for sale and made the deal and returned to England to raise funds to purchase it. A group from England finished the transaction.

Mr. Gordon did not get to return to Israel, but shared the information about the garden and the cistern with his friends. In his drawings he marked the place where they should uncover to look for the garden tomb. His friends came to Israel and found it as he had shown.

When we visited this sacred place, my heart responded, "This is the place where they laid Him." What a worship time we had! On our third trip to the Holy Land, Rev H.E. Schmul and I traveled together and shared rooms. We came from the tomb weeping. There was a place provided for a communion service. It was my privilege to help Rev. Thompson with this worship service. What a blessed time we had. As tears were flowing from Rev. Schmul's eyes, he exclaimed, "Let's sing BECAUSE HE LIVES." He began singing. We joined him and left the communion room singing.

When we stopped our singing, another tour group came down the hill and they were singing the same song, but in another language. We began rejoicing and embracing. We learned they were from Sweden. We were all worshiping the same risen Savior! An experience that will not be forgotten!

As we made out way up the KIDRON VALLEY to OLIVET on one of our journeys, we found that we could still go beneath the olive trees where Jesus prayed. I can say this because we are told the roots of these trees never die. I tarried and prayed in that sacred place.

On the MOUNT OF OLIVES we saw the traditional place of Jesus' Ascension. There is a crack in the mount. It may be a reminder that when Christ returns and sets His feet on the mountain, it will divide asunder. I feel He will be coming soon.

As with the Garden Tomb, there is much to see and tell of the city of JERUSALEM: the Upper Room where we prayed; the Weeping Wall where we saw the Israelite priests pray; following the footsteps of Jesus on the way to the cross. The precious Bible is now more clearly understood. To me Jerusalem is not only the greatest city in the world. I base this on sacred writ. The final redemption events of Jesus' life here on earth took place in Jerusalem.

The SEA OF GALILEE is 13 miles long and 7 miles wide. It is 680 feet below sea level. Because of its place in Bible history, you gain a sacred feeling when looking upon it. I felt it the most beautiful sight in all Israel.

Our group made the voyage across the sea. Since it was hoped to fill the boat with passengers and we were a smaller group than many, we joined with a Catholic Church group from Ireland.

Rev. Robert Thompson was our leader. He came to me and said, "Brother Gale, our guide is not giving lectures about Galilee, so I want you to share 15 minutes with the priest." I went to tell the priest we were to share the time. His reply was, "I bring many groups to Israel. This is a very common experience for me. You take the full 15 minutes."

I prayed silently, "Lord, You must help me. This is an unplanned privilege." I spoke of the fact that many accounts of scripture were connected with Jesus' ministry. As thoughts came to me, I spoke about them. I then told our friends that the sea was not always calm as we were enjoying it.

I cited the time when Jesus was asleep and one of the flash storms struck the sea. The disciples in their fear cried: "'Master, carest thou not that we perish?' and he arose, and rebuked the wind, and said to the sea, 'Peace be still.' And the wind ceased, and there was a great calm" Mark 4:38.39. A special thought came to me. I asked, "Do you realize why Jesus could do that?" Then I answered my own question: "He made the Sea!" The feeling of His almighty power was realized anew in the midst of beautiful Galilee. Catholic and Protestant alike wept together.

When we arrived at the shore, many of the Catholic friends came to thank me for helping them to meet Jesus in a special way upon the Sea. We met on two other occasions in our travel. Each time they would exclaim, "We met Jesus, the all powerful One, on the Sea!" This is a cherished memory.

From Israel, we bused down to Egypt. This large desert area is where Joseph fled with Mary and Baby Jesus to escape Herod. Memphis, the ancient capital of Egypt just south of Cairo, the modern capital, is the traditional place where the Holy family fled. We rode a boat on the Nile River, along whose banks the major life of Egypt is found. We visited many ancient tombs while in this country. My pastor, Rev. Joseph Smith, and his father, Rev. Lewis Smith, were with us on this trip. They are dear friends and it meant much to have their fellowship and to follow the footsteps of Jesus together.

Journeys to Taiwan, Korea, Japan, Mexico, Canada, Hawaii, New Guinea, Guam, the Philippines and others, are places to report in heaven when I have more time!

14

A Home for My Library

Back Row: David Gale, Alice Churchill, Aleta Blue, Dr. Michael Avery, Ruth Avery
Seated: Alice and William Gale

My books mean a great deal to me. Once during the early part of a preaching service, I said in a pleasant, yet teasing way, "If we have a fire at our house, I will hurry and carry out my books. Then I'll go back and get my wife and then my children." With wit and a bit of retaliation, my wife came up to sing and said, "If we have a fire at our house, I'll carry out my piano and then come back for my husband and children." They seemed to enjoy her reply more than my threat.

Through the years I have loved good books. Many times I have spent meal money for a book. I can't be certain, but I believe I have given to others as many books as I have presented to the Gale Mission Study

Center at GBS. I have put forth effort to secure the best sermon material I could afford. I have been privileged to give away many sets of commentaries to friends.

My book shelves are nearly empty, and I have a lonesome feeling. My wife and I have been prayerful in what we have done. We love Bible Colleges. God's Bible School is high on our list. We love the Bible College presidents we know. Dr. Avery is one of our cherished friends. It gives my wife and me great pleasure to know that our library will aid youth in training for the ministry and for missions. There are many special mission books that I did not have. I hope some of these can be added to the Study Library. As to our collection of missionary artifacts, we value them almost equal with our books. Each item has a story to tell. It is our desire that students will sit in a missionary atmosphere and then go forth to reach the lost of earth for Jesus.

Mrs. Mary Nell Vess served the position of Bible Methodist Missions Treasurer when we began serving as General Missions Secretary. Dr. Michael Avery followed her in that position. Both were very helpful to us. We have a big debt to them. They carefully and ably handled the mission funds. Following our tenure, Dr. Avery was elected General Missions Secretary. Now as president of GBS, he is helping us get our life story ready for print.

What we are presenting in this chapter is taken from *God's Revivalist* periodical and from the Dedication Service which was held November 1, 2001. Many will remember that occasion.

William D. Gale Study Center
for
World Missions

God's Bible School and College
Cincinnati, Ohio

Dedicated, November 1, 2001
The Life and Legacy of Dr. William D. Gale

Born in a sod house on a Nebraska ranch in 1920, William Duane Gale has committed his long and colorful life to the cause for redeeming lost humanity. His passion for the lost led to a life of pastoring, twenty-one years on administrative/faculty work in Bible training institutions, twenty-two years of general level denominational leadership, of which fourteen were spent as General Secretary of Foreign Missions. He worked with Brainerd Indian School for fifteen years, nine of which he served as President. His tenure at Brainerd was a time of significant expansion for the school. He was co-founder of the Northwest Indian Bible School and the founder of the Latin American Bible Institute. He was responsible for re-building the college campus of the Philippine Bible Methodist College and extending the work in the Philippines for the Bible Methodists. In sixty years of active ministry, Dr. Gale has given almost forty of those years to some form of missionary activity. He has served the work of missions in the following organizations: The Wesleyan Church, the Allegheny Wesleyan Methodist Church, the Bible Methodist Church, Northwest Indian Bible School, Society of Indian Missions, All Tribes Indian School, Florida Evangelistic Association, and Friends of Missions. During his work among Native Americans, he earned the endearing title of "Chief Hugs Himself" but the church at large refers to him as "Mr. Missions."

God's Bible School, College and Missionary Training Home

Dr. Gale served two terms as a member of the Board of Trustees of God's Bible School and College. He has chosen to place his library and legacy here because at the very heart of our historic vision is a commitment to global missions. That passion has been so forceful through the years that today few institutions can boast of a more glorious history of missionary zeal through its graduates than God's Bible School and College. Our "Missionary Hall of Fame" includes such names as Charles and Lettie Cowman (founders of OMS International), the E.A. Kilbournes (Co-founders of OMS International), Lula Schmelzenbach (Swaziland), Lillian Trasher (Egypt), John Simpson (Philippines), Claudia Peyton (Africa), and Wesley Duewel (India). In more recent years, a few of the names that could be listed are Glenn Pelfrey (Papua New Guinea, Ukraine), Glenn and Helen Reiff (Guatemala, Honduras), Leonard and Janet Sankey (Honduras), Bob and Barbara Brock (Papua New Guinea),

Melvin Adams (Ukraine), Andrea Whiteman (Romania), and Tom and Sharon McKnight (Honduras). Our Missions legacy has been so far-reaching that the Alumni-Association adopted as its motto, "The sun never sets on the students of God's Bible School." Our commitment to missions remains strong as we begin to train missionaries for the new millennium.

Purpose of the Study Center

The William D. Gale Study Center for World Missions will be a "state-of-the-art" classroom and research center to prepare missions majors for the Twenty-first century. It will also serve to honor and preserve the life and legacy of one of our greatest ambassadors for the cause of world missions.

The task of preparing today's missionaries for tomorrow's work cannot be adequately done without keeping before them the legacy and example of yesterday's heroes. The study center will surround our students with the resources to train, while reminding them of a great man who has gone before them.

Funds raised above the amount needed for the library project will go into the William D. Gale Scholarship Fund which will be used for annual awards to qualifying Missions majors.

The long-range plans for this study center will be to re-locate it in a new educational building which will house a center for world missions. The William D. Gale Library and Study Center will be placed in that new building.

Remarks from the Family

I have been appointed to speak on behalf of families of the Reverend Dr. William D. Gale at the occasion of the dedication of the World Missions Study Center, the library and collection of artifacts from around the world that represent the life and times of Rev. and Mrs. William D. Gale. These are today being donated to this institution.

I'm told that when speaking on an occasion like this, there are two things you should accomplish. One, you should always be witty and two, you should be charming, and if you can be neither of those you should be brief. Although it will be difficult, I will attempt to be brief. I shall make every attempt to keep this from sounding like an obituary or a life history.

My father used alliterations in the majority of his sermons over the years. I will attempt to characterize some of the high points of his life in a similar manner. Thus, the reason I can say these remarks are brief as brevity and what my father would call a short sermon are oxymoronic. I fully realize these are filtered and seen by an unbiased party. I will attempt to characterize some of the values that were demonstrated in our home growing up as a child and those that were acquired later in adulthood. I have entitled these remarks "Growing up with William Gale and Paul Harvey."

I grew up with William Gale and Paul Harvey, and any lunch hour conversation had an intermission in it. We could be talking about anything, including solving the world's problems but when my father's clock went off at 12:15 we swallowed our word to hear. "This is Paul Harvey, stand by for News." All thoughts were held until we heard the sign-off Good Day! My father let Paul control the news content and William was responsible for all spiritual applications, even when none were to be found.

In reflecting upon the life and values of William and Alice Gale, one of the values that stand out first in their lives was the role that is played by family. This family is large and extended in many ways. His extended family reaches from coast to coast, from sea to shining sea. He can move around the globe and his extended family is there. I am sure many of you in this audience would consider yourself a part of his family. I shall, however, limit my remarks to the first-degree relatives in deference to both time and the nature of this presentation.

Permit me one observation, as a human geneticist. Some of the family came from the shallow end of the gene pool, others of us came from the deep end of the gene pool, and throughout this day, I will let you make that determination. However, let me resume, what were the characteristics that I viewed were important in the Life of William Gale? The first of these is:

FAMILY

William Gale was born in 1920 in a sod house in the sand hills of Nebraska. He was the third child in a family of eight. Typical of the families of Nebraska, his family was involved in farming, ranching, railroading and the like. As a youngster, he was involved in many of these lifetime activities. His mother was Cynthia, a godly woman, and William

Britt was his father, a good and caring man. William D. was known by many nicknames. I should not spend much time on them, except to acknowledge that one of his favorites was, since his father's name was William, to have been called "Little Bill." Seated in the audience are members of his family and I am going to ask that they will stand and be recognized and that you hold your applause until they have all been acknowledged.

Let me first acknowledge his wife and companion of the past 40 plus years, Alice Jones Gale. She alone merits a place in heaven, a kinder and more loving stepmother for the four Gale children could not have been found. She has stood by my father and served as a role model for the relationship that can only occur between a husband and wife.

His oldest sister Florence Jergensen, known to the family as Aunt Pat, hails now from Tulsa, Oklahoma. She spent most of her adult life in the Gale hometown of North Platte, Nebraska. Seated on the platform is her son Gary, and if you have your golf clubs with you, I can assure you he is ready for nine or 18 holes. Joyce, the third in line of six children, hails from Birmingham, Alabama. Being from the South myself, you will understand that it will not be necessary for you to have an interpreter; she understands proper southern English. I must confess over the years, Joyce was among the favorite of my cousins.

Second in line, is my father's youngest sister, Ruth Kalb and her husband Albert. They have spent much of their lives in various forms of ministry including some time in Sierre Leone, West Africa as missionaries. They have been most recently located at Lindale, Texas and work with the "Sowers." Albert is a minister, educator and Ruth a registered nurse.

Seated with my family are my two sisters. Alice Churchill and her husband Donald Churchill, who is seated on the platform, hail from California. Seated on the platform is Don's younger and much smaller brother Dr. Clifford Churchill. I must pause to acknowledge the hard work of Alice in working to prepare the displays you will be seeing today. She is truly a talented decorator and a lovely older sister. My second and younger sister Aleta Blue is from Wichita, Kansas (Aleta, I must apologize to you, I left the wonderful things you emailed me about you on my computer) and she is accompanied by her youngest son Del Blue. Seated also with the family are daughter Heather and her brother, my son Michael David. We reside in the Commonwealth of Kentucky.

Family is a value firmly held by my father.

FOUNDATION

Over the years, the William Gale family and relatives have recognized in their brother, uncle, father, grandfather, an individual whose basic values are placed on a foundation of high moral principles. I could spend considerable time enumerating these values that serve as the foundation for life choices for William and his family, but I will not. The foundation of God, motherhood and the flag rang out, as does "Old Glory" in the Gale's home.

The third value may strike you as a bit humorous and I hope it will:

FUNNY

My father has been known since his school days as having a real sense of humor, from the time he tied a goat in the top of the silo and harnessed a cow while yet in Bible School, to having some men at Brainerd Indian School dig out old toilet pits, to the myriads of hours he has spent in the playful and gleeful time of having fun for himself and with others. I would suggest to you that an issue of having fun in life is part of a foundational value of William Gale. Now my father has done a lot of this in his life; many of you can repeat the many stories about my father. He has an incredible sense of humor. Both hard work and humor were a big part of his life; as a child I wished we had spent more time with humor and less time with hard work. My father is a masterful storyteller, and he can keep you entertained for hours telling childhood stories. Many of his sermons include considerable story telling, and he has developed this in his ministry to an art form, a quality greatly admired.

FUNDS

Almost his entire lifespan has been spent in raising money for others, the building of churches in Nebraska and South Dakota, the building of schools in South Dakota and Montana, the Philippines, Texas and Mexico. He has given his life and his heart to raising money to bring the ministry and message of Jesus Christ to the world. He forgot to lay up earthly treasures for himself. Dad, I hope the heavenly treasures will feed you when you get old.

FIRM

My father and Paul Harvey set the groundwork for firm beliefs about the way life should be. Again, Monday through Friday, on a daily basis we would pause to hear the words of Paul Harvey and then the contextual applications coming from the Reverend William. My father firmly believes in the scripture, "I will guide thee with mine eye." If you were seated in the audience and for some reason you were not exactly sitting in the straight and narrow upright position, or were found to be whispering, you never wanted that eye to come your way the second time. He has maintained this value, which has not altered in his lifetime.

FINAL

The final chapter of my father's life is now beginning to unfold. It is only now that one looks back to view one's legacy to humanity in order to ascertain and understand the meaning of what we have done with our lives. We know that we have only one life to live and only what is done for Christ will last.

Dr. Avery, as President of God's Bible School and College, on behalf of the Gale Family it is both a privilege and honor to entrust to your care these library and missionary holdings. It is the hope, and the family prays, that lives of young people may be touched through these books and memories. May this day remain as a stepping-stone to take the missionary program of this institution to a higher level of excellence … "That the generations to come might know, even the children yet to be born" Psalms 78:6. It is our family prayer and wish that God's smile and blessing will be present upon this day.

UNCLE WILLIAM

Gail Jergensen (October 13, 2000)

My Uncle's smarter than any uncle is,
And I do mean smart, cuz my unc's a whiz!

Smarter, like Yogi, than a mere average bear
(Smart, like he's smart, is exceedingly rare)

My Uncle knows just all sorts of stuff
Stumpin' my uncle is all kinds of tough.

When wanting opinions and wondering what's nice,
We ask Uncle William; he's full of advice.

In need of assessments too weighty to gauge
We ask Uncle William – the family sage.

If it's about ball games, he's seen the ball bounce,
And he can tell you which teams you can trounce.

If it's about horseshoes, my Uncle's a ringer.
On musical topics, this guy's a (hum)dinger.

On courtship and marriage, he knows what to say
And, just like he calls it, it turns out that way.

On issues of religion it never seems odd
To ask Uncle William, cuz he talks to God.

And then, when God's answer is clear as can be,
'Twill land in a sermon for you and for me.

You ask me, I'll tell you, we think William's grand
There's nary an uncle like him in the land.

So if you face questions both heavy and weighty
Just ask for my Uncle William (who's now more than eighty).

UNCLE WILLIAM'S BOOKS

If anything's smart as my Uncle is
It's got to be them books of his.

And now they're going to college, he said,
So their wisdom can fill someone else's head.

Now I think that's neat! That's really cool –
Giving his books like that to a school!

I hope them kids that study up there
Will remember my Uncle with a Thankful Prayer

And study and learn and answer God's call
To be teachers and preachers, and tell to all –

There's souls to teach and heaven to win,
And there ain't much time if they are gonna get in!

—Gail Jergensen (October 31, 2001)

Written by Gail Jergensen on my 80th birthday with an addition for
Gale Mission Center Dedication at God's Bible School.

Michael Avery, Clifford Churchill, Chris Cravens, David Gale, Joe Smith, Robert Thompson, Don Churchill, Gary Jergensen (Leonard Sankey not pictured)

SPECIAL HONOR COMMITTEE
GALE MISSION STUDY CENTER

Dr. Michael R. Avery	President, GBS
Dr. Leonard Sankey	General Secretary, IHC
Dr. Clifford Churchill	Academic Dean, HSBC
Dr. David D. Gale	Dean, College of Health Sciences, EKU
Mr. Gary Jergensen	Area Director State Farm Insurance
Rev. Joe Smith	Pastor, Bible Holiness Church
Rev. Robert Thompson	Pastor, Bethel Holiness Church
Rev. Chris Cravens	Pastor, Findlay Bible Methodist
Rev. Don Churchill	West Coast Labels

CHAPTER 15
Some Special Incidents

William in Doctoral Robe and Alice Holding Parchment

*S*ome incidents I wish to relate are amusing; others are of honors received.

*   *   *   *   *

When I went to the Telegraph Newspaper office to pick up a cut (illustration for printing) of myself, there was a note attached. It read, "Please come to my office and see me." It was signed "Dick Downing."

He had been a schoolmate of mine. I was glad to see him. He looked at me in wonder and exclaimed, "Red Gale, the last man on earth I ever expected to be a preacher!" Then it was my turn to be surprised. I said, "Dick Downing! I never expected you to be an office manager!" This was an opportunity to tell him I had been converted. I had done a complete turn-around with the Lord's help.

✳ ✳ ✳ ✳ ✳

Robert and Mary Eleanor Carroll were very dear friends of mine. He was my instructor for Greek, Life of Christ and other subjects. The Carrolls did not have a car and I did, so I furnished their transportation lots of times. Mary Eleanor and her two sisters grew up in an orphanage at Mitchell, South Dakota. She and her sister Naomi married the Carroll brothers, Robert and Dick.

Bob told Dick and Mary told Naomi that I was a fun person to travel with. So Dick and Naomi thought it would be interesting to take me with them on their honeymoon. Dick asked me if I would go with them. He told me where they were planning to go. He would pay my meal and hotel expenses. I thought he was joking. I said, "Sure, I'll go if I can sit in the middle." He laughed, but he was serious about my going. I ended up going with them.

I had lots of fun entertaining this young couple. We were about the same age. We went to the St. Louis Zoo. There we saw the Chimpanzee Show, the monkeys riding on ponies and the great Lion Act. I had never been to a zoo, had never stayed in a hotel, nor had I ever eaten big meals in a restaurant. Many things we enjoyed. I almost decided to take this up for a life's occupation.

✳ ✳ ✳ ✳ ✳

Alice Kathryn Jones came to Brainerd Indian School as an elementary school teacher in the fall of 1957. She held this position four school terms: 1957-1961. In the spring of 1961 Alice and I were married. She was chosen "Teacher of the Year" and was featured in the South Dakota State Teachers' Journal for the 1958-1959 school year. As a staff we were all proud of her. She put us on the map! The Iowa Achievement Tests were given at the beginning of the year and then again at the closing. Her students showed the greatest gains of all elementary students in the state.

She has been working hard to help one dull scholar now for 42 years. She perhaps hopes he can graduate soon.

* * * * *

Rev. J.D. Young and some of my preacher friends of the Ohio Conference wanted to do something in my honor. They arranged with a college to give me an Honorary Doctor of Divinity Degree and they, along with Dr. Leslie Wilcox, conferred it. My family purchased a beautiful black robe with red velvet trim for the occasion. This special honor of distinction was a surprise, but very meaningful since those men with whom I labored felt I deserved the honor.

* * * * *

There have been times when special words of appreciation and confidence have boosted my morale and made me want even more to be a blessing in my ministry. My wife has told me that she likes my preaching and that I feed her spiritually from the Word. That was better than a meal! I have loved it when children wrote little love notes or came to tell me they liked my preaching. I wish I had kept the notes. I would put them in this book.

I was preaching a revival and a saintly lady seemed startled that I came to shake her hand. She said, "Rev. Gale, your kind spirit is the kind I think Jesus has." This was Mrs. Hill, the mother of Mrs. Nancy Feracioly. I had been discouraged and wanted to be kinder. Across the years, seasoned saints have lifted my spirit.

* * * * *

I was very sick and in the hospital at Hot Springs, South Dakota. I was president of Brainerd Indian School at the time. Four students from our Bible Department came to my room: Earl Beare, Donald John, Jerry Yellowhawk and Leroy Rattling Leaf. Two stood on one side of my bed and two on the other. Jerry said, "We came to pray." His prayer was, "Dear Lord, here is one white man who loves us Indians. He is sick and we are strong. We are asking you to take this sickness from him and put it on us." I loved them so much for praying that way. I felt their love, but then I prayed, "Don't do it, Lord, don't do it." Then they slipped out of the room.

They didn't know it, but three Indian mothers had been in to see me a little while before. All three had young people in our school. Mrs. Kills Back was one of the mothers. They didn't say a word, but just lined up across the room and stood there wiping tears from their eyes. Mrs. Kills Back squeezed my big toe through the sheet as they left the room.

Now with four choice young men who had all been remarkably converted and three concerned mothers caring, I got out of my bed and called the nurse to get my clothes. I told her I would take care of it with Dr. Roper and the hospital. There were those who loved me and I had to get well and get out of there. By the time I reached the sidewalk outside the hospital, I was well.

✳ ✳ ✳ ✳ ✳

I want to report an incident that occurred on my pastorate at Niobrara, Nebraska. One day our Sunday School Superintendent said to me, "Rev. Gale, if you really want to see our Sunday School grow, you need to get my brother-in-law, Charley Gatz converted." I told her I would try.

I started visiting their home. I told Mrs. Gatz I had come to see her husband. She told me he had seen me coming and slipped out the back door. I visited a bit with her and left. When I called the next time, I knocked at the back door, but he went out the front door. He wouldn't have a thing to do with me. His wife told me that Charlie accused her of having an affair with the preacher although he knew that wasn't true. The next time I took my wife with me. Mrs. Gatz thanked me for coming, but said it would be best if I didn't call on them. This was a blow I didn't expect, but I fasted and prayed about the situation.

One day Gail Ellingson phoned and said, "Pastor, I need some help. I need sand for cement work and there is only one man to help me." I told him I could help. He said he'd be by to pick me up in 15 minutes. By the time I got into work clothes, they had arrived. When I opened the truck door, I saw the other man was Charley Gatz. I got in and shut the door. Charley was mad. He jabbed his elbow into my side. It hurt so bad I wanted to scream. He wouldn't speak to me. I talked to Gail over the top of Charley.

Gail said we needed to remove the top soil from an area and then scoop the sand into the truck. When we got to the place, I opened the door and Charley shoved me so hard that he fell over the top of me. He grabbed a spade and started shoveling the top soil. I grabbed a spade and threw a shovel full of soil every time Charley did. It wasn't long until Gail said, "We have enough uncovered now so we can throw sand into the truck." I threw a shovel full every time Charley did. Gail finally said, "The truck springs are about completely down. This is a big load." When we were going through town, Charley got out and said, "I'll see you in a little while."

Gail went to his parents' house to see about something. They both showed up when I got the truck unloaded. When we got back to the sand area, Charley didn't let up a bit. We scooped sand like crazy. Finally, Gail said, "We have a load." They both did a repeat when we got to town. Charley got off in town and Gail went to the house on business. I unloaded the second truck load and they both showed up again. Gail said, "One more load." My back and arms complained that two loads were enough. We had the third load on when Charley said, "We don't have to work so fast!" I said, "I've been thinking that for quite a while."

After we sat and rested, he said, "Preacher, did you ever saw wood?" I said, "Some." He said, "Why don't we cut up our winter fuel supply together?" I asked, "Charley, do you saw wood like you scoop sand?" He smiled and replied, "Preacher I have never had a man out work me before and to think a preacher did it." We finished our load. Charley and I sawed and cut up our winter fuel supply.

He declared far and near that I was the best preacher in the country. I did ask him about his family coming to church. He said, "They will all be there Sunday. I'll see to it." He helped our church to grow more than any of our members. He said, "Come to our home any time you want to." Charley never came to hear me preach. I ate many meals in their home. I loved him and prayed for him. He went about telling people of my qualities.

We moved to another pastorate. He was often on my mind. One day the phone rang. Mrs. Gatz was calling. Charley told her to phone me and tell me that he was lonesome for me and his home was always open to me. He had also said, "Tell Preacher Gale I just got saved!" It is 4:35 A.M. I am weeping. I'll need to finish this chapter after a while. I should say to you Christian workers that there is often a price to pay to win men and women to the Lord.

* * * * *

We wrote of our trip to Alaska with John and Yvonne Betters. There was a special happening I would like to report. In making plans for the trip, I told the Betters that we would take our car and pay for the gasoline. Occasionally, Rev. Betters would ask me if I had received anything to help pay our travel expenses. I had to say that I hadn't.

We were now in the car and nearly ready to begin our journey back home. John Betters said, "This is our last stop until we get home. Have you got any money yet?" I said, "No, but the trip isn't over yet." Ida May Merrill was not within hearing distance of our conversation. She came over to the car and said, "Just a minute." She came back and slipped $400.00 worth of $20.00 bills to me. This was the amount we needed. Both my wife and I had to gulp to hold back the tears.

* * * * *

On a recent trip to Alaska where I spoke in a big log church in Fairbanks, I saw Gladys Main and Ida May Merrill. Gladys was 94 years of age. She reminded me of the time she gave me a negative pastoral vote. I had decided if one voted that way, there may be others that would wish for a change, also. Sunday morning I resigned in honor of that one vote. The church board got up in arms and asked me to meet with them. Gladys told me she cast a negative vote because she felt the church was taking advantage of my kindness, but if I felt I should stay, she would change her vote.

When Reverend Betters asked whether she would be coming to hear me at the recent Inter-Church Holiness Convention at Fairbanks, her reply was, "Coming? I should say so. William Gale was my former pastor and favorite preacher." The Christian bonds are very strong. Gladys Main is a great saint and a true-blue friend!

CHAPTER 16

The End of the Trail

William and Alice

"The End of the Trail" is the title James Earl Frazier gave to his sculpture of the North American Indian. This art production was made when he was seventeen years of age. The much larger and final model made by Frazier has been placed in the Indian Room of the Cowboy Hall of Fame at Oklahoma City, Oklahoma. Both James and his wife Laura were famous sculptors. His

"End of the Trail" production won first prize at an art exhibit in Paris. He wrote the following to a friend:

"Your letter of inquiry in regard to my statue, *The End of the Trail,* came to me yesterday. This is its history: As a small boy living in the South Dakota Territory, I came in close contact with the Sioux Indians. The period was from 1880 to 1888 … played with the Indian children and liked their games very much. Often hunters, wintering with the Indians, stopped over to visit my Grandfather on their way South, and in that way I heard many of their stories.

"On one occasion a fine, fuzzy-bearded, old hunter remarked, with much bitterness in his voice, 'The Injuns will all be driven into the Pacific Ocean.' The thought so impressed me that I couldn't forget it; in fact, it created a picture in my mind which eventually became *The End of the Trail* … I made many sketches and some finished work, and at the age of seventeen, in 1894, I created the first model of *The End of the Trail,* the thought that had been in my mind since my boyhood in Dakota."

I have two cherished paintings. One was painted by Lyle High Pipe; the other by Jerry Yellowhawk. Both of these talented artists are Sioux Indians. These paintings are displayed on the walls of our "Indian Room" at Edinburgh, Indiana.

Lyle's grandmother was converted in a revival we were holding at Mission, South Dakota. This painting was a gift to us and depicts a scene from the Bad Lands of South Dakota. The horse is standing behind his rider, who is seated at the very edge of the cliff. The horse's head is bent low and as you look at the painting, you are made to feel the utter hopelessness of both horse and rider.

Jerry Yellowhawk's painting is called "The Trail's End." He featured an Appaloosa horse (a breed developed by the Nez Perce Indian tribe). In the painting, the horse's head hangs low over the edge of the cliff and the Indian is sitting in a slumped position. Two steps more and both the horse and rider would plunge to their death. You can feel their extreme exhaustion as you gaze at the painting. At my request, the worn-out Indian has a small war shield and a bow with quiver of arrows. This is different from the sculpture's spear, but is very true to life.

I have a very special tie with Jerry and Johanna Yellowhawk since I performed their wedding ceremony. They were students at Brainerd

Indian School and we traveled many, many miles together in mission services.

James Earl Frazier's sculpture is of an Indian on a weary, worn horse. He sits with his head bowed down and the horse's head is bent low. Paintings of the "The End of the Trail" also picture an Indian on his horse. The Indian sags and the horse is fagged out. Painters give a sad portrayal of horse and rider.

I am sitting in my home with a picture of the sculpture "The Trail's End" and also the painting of "The End of the Trail" in my mind. I, too, am bent over, head down in prayer and in weariness. I am writing at age 83. For 62 years of my life, much of my time has been spent educating and training Indian youth. Much time has also been devoted to evangelism of the American Indian.

I feel I am at "The Trail's End" or at "The End of the Trail." My body sags and my head hangs down. Where has time gone so quickly? I have prayed many times, "Lord, send a revival to the American Indian before Jesus comes again." Will the Indian experience that revival? In writing my life story, I review both sorrow and happiness. The Native American has been next to my own family as my chief concern and burden. In my book, *I Sat Where They Sat*, I included the following poem:

The Trail's End

An artist took his brush and paint
And portrayed an Indian dazed and faint.
The picture painted, your heart would rend
Featuring an Indian at "The Trail's End."

The pony stands with head bent low,
His frame so thin it has lost its go;
The Indian rider without a sound
Slumps forward staring at the ground.

The picture reminds me of a story read
Of an Indian Chief who sorrowfully said,
"Missionary, we come with a heavy load
We've reached the end of the Indian road."

His tear-dimmed eyes with distant look
Told of the life he had partook
He continued his words with deep despair,
"The Indian road led to nowhere."

"The Trail's End" picture and words of the chief
Cause me to tremble with heartfelt grief,
Remembering our Lord's commission given
To map the road that leads to heaven.

Dear Lord, I pray as I come to Thee,
In your own clear way speak to me,
And bring a revival to our Indian Friend
Who's dazed and faint at "The Trail's End."

When I was president of Brainerd Indian School, the students gave me the name "Chief Hugs Himself." When I really get amused, I tend to hug myself.

In approaching my trail's end, I look back on a happy life of service for my Lord. At present, I still hold my head up. The Lord who saved me has filled my heart with joy. My trail has led to many mission fields around the world.

Mary Alice for 19 years and Alice Kathyrn for 42 years have journeyed by my side. David and Donald and Alice and Aleta accompanied us to regions round and about. We have been a happy family. The children are in their own homes now and Mary Alice and Donald are in heaven. Alice and I have been in all the states of the USA, most of the provinces of Canada, and states of Mexico. We have loved friends in most every port. With heads held high, we both have fond memories of being astraddle steeds, riding in buggies, in buckboards, buses, boats, cars, planes and even bikes.

Our future looks bright. The Lord has said to us, "Let not your heart be troubled: ye believe in God believe also in me. In my Father's house are many mansions; if it were not so, I would have told you. I go to prepare a place for you. And if I go and prepare a place for you, I will come again and receive you unto myself; that where I am there ye may be also" (John 14:1-3). This will be our final flight.

Revelation 19:11, 14 describes our Lord: "And I saw heaven opened; and behold a white horse and he that sat upon him was called Faithful and True. And the armies which were in heaven followed him upon white horses, clothed in fine linen, white and clean."

We have no way to know how Jesus will take us to the White City when He comes back to earth for His own. When He does come forth upon the white horse, His vesture is dipped in blood and His name is called the Word of God. We hope to ride again upon white horses clothed in fine linen white and clean. "The End of the Trail."